The not so roman

Written by Andy Lickley

Independently published in Great Britain 2022.

Copyright 2022 by Andrew Lickley

Andrew Lickley asserts the moral right to be identified as the author of this work.

No part of this book may be used or reproduced in any manner whatsoever without written permission from the author except in the case of brief quotations embodied in critical articles or reviews.

ISBN: 9798799023300

Before we begin…

As you may or may not know I self-published this book. This means that I don't have a big publishers marketing team to help me promote it.

I need your help! Once you've finished the book, please leave an honest review on the book's Amazon page. The more reviews there, the more likely people who stumble across the book are to buy it.

The more reviews the higher up Amazons search page the book will be. By leaving a review, not only for this book, but for my other self-published works, it gives them a much bigger chance of being discovered. I certainly appreciate every review I receive.

So please take a little bit of time out of your day to leave an honest review. (Don't feel you have to put 5 stars or anything. If you thought it was a 3-star book, then review it as 3 stars). Honest reviews are the most important.

Word of mouth is also incredibly important so please, if you know anyone else who would enjoy this book encourage them to check it out. You could maybe even lend them this book!

If there is anything you can do to promote this book and help achieve my dream of being a fulltime author, then I will be the most grateful person on the planet.

Andy

This book is dedicated to my favourite person – who, for purpose of suspense and mystery, will remain nameless.

Hello! And welcome to the not so romantic railways.

The first thing I did when starting to write this book was ask people a simple question.

"What do you imagine when someone says the word railways?"

Some people told me about the many delays they experience when travelling on the trains.
Other people told me how some people on the train smelt like they didn't know how to shower.
Then someone told me that the railways were romantic.
I admit I dropped my strawberry flavoured Slush Puppy when I heard this.

The railways were romantic....

I've been on trains enough to know they get delayed, and my nose has been on the receiving end of badly washed people but were the railways romantic?
The person who insisted the railways were romantic meant a different generation of the railways.

The generation of steam.

When people say the railways were romantic, they don't mean that the locomotives bought everyone flowers and chocolate and treated their crew to candlelit dinners or romantic walks in the country.
When people say the railways were romantic, they are talking about the sights, smells, the colours, the journeys, and sounds.

The more I thought about it the more I realised I had an issue with the railways being known as romantic. Mostly because it's a big, fat, not very attractive lie.

You have probably already noticed that this book is called the "not so romantic railways." And it's called that for a really good reason.

In this book I'm going to take you all the way back to the Victorian era (1837-1901) and I'm going to tell you exactly why the railways weren't romantic.

I'm going to tell you the stories history has forgotten about. Some of the stories are funny, some are a little scary, some are educational, and some are just stupid. My promise to you is that each and every story in this book is true.

Before we get started, I should introduce myself...

My name is Andy, and I spent a long time working in the learning team at the National Railway Museum in York. During this time, I unearthed and discovered lots of stories, facts and figures about the railways. It was my job to know as much as possible about the railways. I'm often surprised how much I do know.

I'm not silly enough to pretend I know everything about the railways, but I definitely know more than your average rhinoceros.

To prove to you that I know what I'm talking about let's start with a fact.

The world's fastest steam engine is called Mallard. It travelled 126 miles per hour back in 1938.

Impressive fact, right? I know what you're thinking though. Anyone with an internet connection could find that out.

How about this one...

THE TEACHERS ARE WRONG

A lot of teachers will tell you that Stephenson's Rocket was the first steam locomotive ever built. This is wrong! Zero points rewarded. The first steam locomotive was actually built by Richard Trevithick in 1804.

With that fact you can correct your teachers. Don't be too mean though, we don't want to make them cry. In fact, if you're just here to try and prove that your teacher doesn't know anything about the railways, there's a whole section at the back of the book dedicated to teachers are wrong facts.

WARNING!

There is an extremely large chance you might learn something when reading this book. Please don't hate me if you do.

I think that's enough from me for now though.

Welcome everyone to,,,

THE NOT SO ROMANTIC RAILWAYS

Contents

A brief timeline	12
Rocket and the Rainhill trails	15
How a steam locomotive works	28
Jobs	36
The fireman's shovel	42
Where does the poo go?	46
The fussy Queen	55
The travelling post office	62
Snack break!	65
The first railway murder	69
The great gold robbery	76
London Underground	83
Daddy long legs	86
Trains of the dead	89
Armagh rail disaster	92
Brilliant Brunel's	96
Charles Dickens and the Staplehurst rail crash	101
I'm out of chapter titles	104
People you should know	111
Teachers are wrong	129
The locomotives in this book	132
Big fancy words and what they mean.	134

A brief timeline

Pre-Victorian

1771- Richard Trevithick is born.

1781- George Stephenson is born.

1800- George Hudson is born.

1801- Richard Trevithick builds a steam carriage called the Puffing Devil. It explodes after he crashes into a ditch.

1804- Richard Trevithick builds a steam locomotive called the Penydarren, it ran for 9 miles. // Robert Stephenson is born.

1806- Isambard Kingdom Burnel is born.

1808- Richard Trevithick opens his steam circus and builds a locomotive called Catch-me-who-can. It hits a speed of 12 miles per hour!

1812- Charles Dickens is born.

1815- George Stephenson invents the miners safety lamp.

1819- Victoria is born.

1825- The first ever passenger pulling railway opens between Stockton and Darlington.

1829- Rocket wins the Rainhill trials.

1836- George Stephenson is named "father of the locomotive".

Victorian

1837- Queen Victoria is crowned Queen.

1838- London to Birmingham railway opens.

1840- Queen Adelaide becomes the first member of the Royal family to travel by train.

1842- Queen Victoria travels by train for the first time.

1843- Ada Lovelace creates the first complex computer code // Charles Dickens publishes 'A Christmas Carol' and it sells out in six days!

1844- Nearly 5000 miles of track has been built in Britain and George Hudson becomes the Railway king!

1850- There are now roughly 200 railway companies in the country.

1851- The Great Exhibition takes place- this is perhaps the first world's fair type event in the world.

1854- London's necropolis railway is opened.

1855 – The great gold train robbery happens.

1859- The origin of species by Charles Darwin is published.

1860- The first fish and chip shop is opened.

1861- Prince Albert dies.

1863- The first underground is opened in London between Paddington and Farrington.

1864- The first railway murder // Clifton Suspension bridge opens.

1868- The last public hanging.

1871- George Hudson dies.

1876- Alexander Graham Bell makes the first ever phone call.

1879- The Tay Bridge collapses.

1880- Education becomes compulsory for children under 10.

1883- The first electric railway in the UK.

1887- Queen Victoria's golden jubilee.

1897- First female murdered on the railways.

1899- Armagh rail disaster.

1901- Queen Victoria dies and Edward becomes king.

Rocket and the Rainhill Trials

Please don't tell anyone but we're going to start with a tale about something that happened a few years before Queen Victorias bottom sat upon the throne. We're going back to 1829 to the Northern city of Liverpool.

A 30-mile canal route connected Liverpool to Manchester. It was used to transport cotton from the ports of Liverpool to the factories in Manchester. 30-miles may not seem like very far, but it took the canal boats 36 hours (1 ½ days) to travel it. That means they were travelling less than one mile per hour. You could walk the 30 miles Manchester, or Liverpool I suppose, quicker than the canal boats.

This wasn't any good for business. So, the decision was made that a railway line would be built to improve delivery times.

I'd like to introduce you to someone now- his name was George Stephenson. You may have already heard of him. In most history books he's called the "father of the railways". Teachers and most railway people love him. Everyone sings his praises and describes him in such a way that makes you think he sneezed solid gold bogies. I'm confident most people think his trumps smelt like roses and his burps sounded like angels singing.

I'm sorry to be the one to do it- but I'm going to burst that little "all hail George Stephenson" bubble. He probably isn't as great as everyone says he is, and his trumps certainly didn't smell like roses. Actually, I can't state the trumps thing as fact as I never smelt any of them, so maybe they did smell like roses.

Sorry to all you George Stephenson fans- this next bit may be a little difficult to read.

When the nice folks of the newly formed Liverpool and Manchester Railway board decided to build a railway track, they turned to angel burps George Stephenson for help. To build a railway you first surveyed the land to plot the best route for your railway and work out how much it would cost to make.

You then took these plans to parliament where they asked you lots of questions and if they were satisfied, they'd let you build the railway. Parliament never paid for the railways to be built as there was plenty of rich people willing to finance them. This is also why the Victorian railway map started off all over the place. People would build their railway at a strange angle in order to literally cut off the competition.

Stephenson took charge of the survey for the Liverpool to Manchester railway and in 1825, the year he opened the famed Stockton and Darlington railway, he went to parliament and for lack of a better word messed it up. He was unable to answer very simple questions and the idea of the Liverpool to Manchester railway was dismissed- good job "father of the railways". Many people put this down to the fact that George's son, Robert Stephenson, was in South America at the time.

Robert Stephenson was the businessmen of the father and son team. Whereas George couldn't read or write Robert could. Because of his education many think if Robert had delivered the survey to parliament, then the bill would have been passed straight away.

Oh! If you were wondering what I'm talking about when I'm talking about a bill. I don't mean them horrible things you have to pay for electric and internet- I'm talking about parliamentary bills. They sound big and fancy but really are just how people propose new laws and other things like railways.

Like a football manager Stephenson was ungracefully sacked and replaced on the project. John and George Rennie completed the survey and when the company returned to parliament in 1826 the bill passed thanks to the work of Stephenson's replacements. This is where George Stephenson got lucky.

Rather than sticking with John and George to build the track for the Liverpool to Manchester railway, the board asked the Stephenson's to build it instead.

Robert returned from South America and, along with his dad, they set about building the 35-mile length track between Liverpool and Manchester. The Stephenson's (not just George) proved themselves great problem solvers when it came to building over a large swamp land called "Chat moss".

The land was swampy so any tracks placed on the ground would sink and you'd end up with an extremely muddy train. Predicting a cleaner's riot if all the trains came back covered in swamp dirt, the Stephenson's' first plan was to try and drain the swamp. This was a silly idea as it would never have worked.

To solve the problem of a sinking railway they created a new base of wood, dirt and stones and kept going until they became strong and non-sinking foundations to build the railway across. It's all still there today so problem solved.

But what was going to run on the Liverpool to Manchester railway? There were many people who wanted horse drawn trains to run the railway. It's a fair argument as horses had run the earliest railway systems for 100 years. Plus, horses are a lot less likely to blow up.

Railways were still a very new and a very uncertain invention. The Stockton and Darlington railway had opened in 1825 but there was still only around 100 miles of track in the whole country.

To find who should be running the soon to be Liverpool to Manchester railway a competition was pulled together to decide if steam locomotives really were the future, and that competition was called the Rainhill trials.

Five engines took part in October 1829, there was a sixth entrant from America which dropped out before the start. You may already know which locomotive won. But let's meet all the competitors.

Cycloped

Designed by Thomas Shaw Brandreth, Cycloped was a horse on a treadmill. The idea was that the horse would run on the treadmill which would drive wheels around. It was the only competitor which wasn't steam powered to take part in the Rainhill trials. There are some suggestions that Cycloped was nothing more than a joke to entertain the crowd as in the Rainhill trials rulebook the locomotives had to be steam powered.

It did reach a dazzling speed of five miles per hour. But the horse had to keep stopping for food and, perhaps more importantly, the horse was too heavy for the treadmill so kept falling through it. This wouldn't have done much for the horse's self-esteem.

It would have been a shock if Brandreth had decided to use a different animal. Imagine an elephant charging down the track on a treadmill?

Novelty

Novelty was built by John Ericsson and John Braithwaite who both had recent history in building steam powered fire engines Novelty was the crowd's favourite to win. If you were to ask the crowd who they thought would win, they would say Novelty. The public trusted it as it looked most similar to a steam carriage and it's highly likely that Novelty was actually a converted fire engine the pair had previously built.

But sadly, quite a lot went wrong with Novelty. Bits kept breaking and no matter how many repairs they made they couldn't keep it running. It was the first locomotive to be tested and in fairness it did reach speeds of around 28mph- but botch repairs could only get them so far before it all went wrong. The final nail in the coffin was when it's water pipe burst.

In fairness there were no railways in London where Novelty was built so they do have a fair excuse as they were unable to properly test the locomotive. If you're ever invited to a race, make sure you can go somewhere to practice first.

Novelty did win the honour of being the first tank locomotive though as it carried water on the actual locomotive, not in a tender behind.

There was some suggestion from Novelty's designers that it had been the first steam powered vehicle to reach 60mph in tests which happened after the Rainhill trials. I'm a little dubious about this- mostly because it only hit 28mph in the actual trails. It doesn't mean it definitely didn't happen; it just seems a little unlikely- I'll leave you to make your own decision though.

Perseverance

Perseverance was built in Scotland by John Reed Hill and Timothy Burstall. Back in 1829 there were no railways track between Scotland and Liverpool, so Perseverance was loaded onto a reliable horse and cart.

The horse and cart may have been reliable, but the roads were so bumpy Perseverance fell off the cart several times. But the biggest fall actually came once they'd made it to the race site when the unloaders were careless.

This meant Perseverance was out before the race had even begun. It was the railway equivalent of falling and breaking your leg on the way to the start line.

Sans Pareil

Sans Pareil was built by Timothy Hackworth who was no stranger to the Stephenson's. He was actually employed by them; he took over Robert Stephenson's job when Robert went to South

America in 1824. He was responsible for keeping all the locomotives in working order.

He was really important to the building of Locomotion no. 1 which ran on the Stockton and Darlington railway in 1825. The Stockton and Darlington was the first passenger railway to open; George Stephenson has been given nearly all the credit for this momentous moment in history.

The Stephenson's didn't pay Hackworth a massive wage, and he had 7 children in education, and he needed to feed them, so he didn't have massive resources to build his locomotive with. He was given permission to build Sans Pereil in Shildon works- providing he didn't neglect his day job of keeping all the locomotives running on the Stockton and Darlington railway.

Hackworth dedicated himself to his work nobly, but the problem was he didn't have much time to be able to test Sans Pareil before the Rainhill Trials. Testing is a huge part of the engineering process- actually it's a huge part of any process. If you want to learn to bake a cake you don't just make the perfect cake on your first attempt. You bake a cake, learn, bake another cake, learn, bake another cake and so on. Replace "baking a cake" with anything you're trying to accomplish, and you have yourself a recipe for success.

During the race itself Sans Pareil went over the weight limit so wasn't allowed to win the trails. It still ran on the line but was already disqualified. The valves did fail on the locomotive as well and there are suggestions that the makers of the valves were the Stephenson's. Had they sabotaged their competition?

In truth there had been lots of valves made by lots of different companies so it would be impossible to know if the valves which had failed had been made by the Stephenson's. I'll let you decide for yourself if you think it was sabotage.

Even though Sans Pareil didn't win the Rainhill Trials, the Liverpool to Manchester railway company still bought the locomotive and it ran on the line until 1831 before being loaned to other companies. Sans Pareil had a very successful 15-year career.

After the trials Hackworth continued to work for the Stephenson's until 1833 when he packed his bags and formed his own company.

Rocket

So, the winner, mostly by default, was the Rocket! It reached a dazzling speed of 30 miles per hour which was so fast people thought their heads would fall off if they travelled on it. I'm sure everyone here has been 30 miles per hour before and if you are able to read this, I'm guessing your head didn't fall off- unless you're reading this really far in the future and humans have evolved not to have a head. Perhaps the future humans have eyes under their armpits?

I'm actually really disappointed people weren't more creative with their fears of what would happen if you travelled at 30 miles per hour.

If I had the ability to travel back in time, I'd travel back to 1829 and start a rumour that if you travelled at 30 miles per hour your belly button would fall off.

Actually! I have a better idea.

I'd start a rumour that if you travelled at 30 miles per hour bogies would constantly fall out of your left nostril.

What rumour would you spread if you could travel back in time?

And another question, why am I writing 30 miles per hour so many times?

As amusing as the train of thought (that was a joke- did you laugh?) is, let's get back to Rocket...

One of the main reasons to Rocket's success was something called the blast pipe (don't panic I'm not going to bore you with technical detail).

The blast pipe sits underneath the chimney of the locomotive and helps create a bigger draught (air flow) in the firebox to make the fire hotter. Hotter fire means steam being made quicker. The blast pipe had been put on a locomotive called "Royal

George" in 1827 by Timothy Hackworth. What do you think the chances are that the Stephenson's stole the idea of the blastpipe from Hackworth?

In the Stephenson's defence, Hackworth may have stolen the basic from of the idea from someone called Richard Trevithick so they're all as bad as each other. Hackworth probably improved the idea first suggested by Trevithick and then the Stephenson's took it from Hackworth and made a couple of tweaks here and there. Imagine if they'd all worked as a team!

Another reason for Rocket's success was the number of boiler tubes. The boiler tubes carry the hot air made by the fire into the boiler to heat up and boil the water. Most of the early steam locomotives only had one or two tubes of hot air to boil their water. Rocket had 25. You don't need to be a genius to realise that the locomotive boiler will get hotter much faster with more tubes.

At last- something that proves the genius of George Stephenson because surely, he thought up the idea of adding more boiler tubes. Actually, no. The idea came from someone called Henry Booth- a man quite often missed out of the Rainhill Trial story. Booth was the treasurer of the railway. The list of things that George Stephenson didn't invent is quickly growing- can you believe he didn't invent the hairbrush either. Lyda Newman invented what we now recognise as a hairbrush in 1898 - I should also say that Lyda is not a typo.

Rockets builders, Robert, and George Stephenson alongside the forgettable Henry Booth -the man everyone seems to forget about- won a cheque for £500 (about £40,000 today!) and won the rights to run the Liverpool to Manchester railway.

But winning the Rainhill trials meant more for the Rocket. Rocket went onto influence the future generation of steam engines. Rocket was the 1830s equivalent of a modern-day influencer – if I'm influencing people that the railways weren't romantic, does that mean I'm an influencer as well?

Nowadays technology is getting smaller and smaller but back then technology got bigger and bigger. But no matter how big the steam locomotives got they all contained the same technology that Rocket had back in 1829- just with some improvements and additions here and there.

One of the best additions for the later steam locomotives were brakes. That's right, Rocket was built without brakes. In today's health and safety world that seems ludicrous but being able to easily stop the loco wasn't a requirement.

Plus, nobody else had invented it on a steam locomotive so perhaps that's why George Stephenson didn't include them on Rocket. (ooo burn)

Rocket not having brakes proved a very serious problem on the opening of the Liverpool to Manchester railway on the 15th of September 1830.

A member of parliament for Liverpool called William Huskisson was among one of the many guests to be invited to the line's opening. Railway openings back then were really just an excuse for a big party.

When the city of York got their first railway in 1839 the mayor at the time, George Hudson, held a three-day party. Sadly, there was no jelly and ice cream. They did play pin the carriage on the locomotive though.

Anyway...

When they opened the Liverpool to Manchester railway all the important people of the day were invited to ride on the train. On the guest list was the prime minister of the time the "Duke of Wellington" (Arthur Wellesley) and a guy called Steve.

The plan for the opening was simple, take one of the eight trains from Liverpool to Manchester depending on the colour of your ticket.

I should explain actually.

There were eight trains prepared for the opening of the line. And each of them was allocated a different colour. Guests knew which train they were riding behind by the colour of ticket they received. The colour of the ticket would match a flag on one of the locomotives.

Northumbria- Lilac

Phoenix (My nephew's name- I know it's not possible but this locomotive was named after him)- Green

North Star- Yellow

Dart- Purple

Comet- Deep red

Arrow- Pink (The best colour)

Meteor- Brown

One thing all the important people were told was not to get off the train when they stopped to refuel. So, what do you think all the important people did when the trains stopped to refuel?

You guessed it.

They sat in their carriages like they were told and waited for the trains to be refuelled.

Just kidding...

Of course, they all got out their carriages and decided to have a chit-chat on the tracks. You don't need to be very intelligent to realise that having a chit-chat on the tracks was a ludicrous idea.

Their only defence (and it's a weak one) is that steam locomotives were still very new. People were used to horses and a horse can stop quickly and easily change direction to avoid a collision. These are two things steam locomotives can't do. -Locos can't neigh either and don't like polos.

It goes without saying but never go on the railway tracks- no matter what the situation! If the £1,000 fine doesn't put you off, then just remember that if you get hit by a train the bits that are left of you will fit inside a shoebox.

William Huskisson wanted to go shake the Prime Ministers hand so strolled across the track to say hello. The Prime Minister was still in his carriage, so it probably looked like they were re-enacting Romeo and Juliet.

As the two were chatting Rocket - there is no real proof it was actually Rocket, but we'll use a little poetic licence- started to come down the track everyone was stood on.

Everyone scattered back to their carriages and Huskisson was almost across the line and out of danger when for some reason he panicked and turned back. He climbed up the side of the prime minister's carriage, but the door hadn't been latched so instead of providing safety the door swung out in front of Rocket- Huskisson clinging on the side.

Rocket smashed into the door, knocking Huskisson to the ground where his leg was run over.

You know what he said?

"Ouch." (He might have said some more naughty words as well.)

The crew used a door as a makeshift stretcher and George Stephenson himself drove Huskisson to the vicarage in Eccles. Cutting off Huskisson leg wasn't possible, so they made him as comfortable as possible, and he died several hours later.

Huskisson had actually been told by a doctor not to attend the opening of the Liverpool to Manchester railway because of recent medical surgery. Huskisson ignored the advice and wound-up dead. Morale of the story? Listen to your doctor – actually the morale of the story is don't go on the tracks.

Obviously having someone die on the opening of the first inter-city railway was not the best advertisement for the railways and certainly would have added to the growing concern about the steam monsters. Luckily people have short memories.

Rocket went onto have four fairly successful years of service on the Liverpool to Manchester line. In 1834 it underwent some not-so-successful new design tests which can only be called an £80 waste of money. I suppose you could compare it to most people's gym memberships nowadays.

In 1836 it was sold for an impressive sum of £300 and began its new life on the Brampton Railway. The Brampton Railway transported coal from Tindale to Brampton

Rocket pulled coal trucks until 1862 when it was donated to the patent office museum in London. The patent office has a new name nowadays. It's now the Science Museum where Rocket remained for 156 years before going to the National Railway Museum in York, via Manchester.

How a steam locomotive works

Because we're talking about the era of steam it makes sense for me to explain how a steam locomotive works. I apologise because if you're going to learn anything in this book, it is going to be in this chapter.

In my experience steam locomotives are one of those subjects that everyone makes out to be more complicated than it actually is. Those who try to explain it pride themselves on knowing all the complex parts and knowing exactly how many bolts it takes to hold a boiler together.

The biggest problem is that people use far too many big and complicated words. That is one thing I refuse to do. I hate using any big or fancy words, mostly because I don't understand them myself.

Our lesson in how a steam locomotive works starts with a short and very simple sentence.

A steam locomotive is a large kettle on wheels

Obviously if you were to put a kettle and a steam locomotive next to each other, you wouldn't need me to tell you that there are a lot more parts on a steam locomotive than there are on a kettle.

But they both do pretty much the same thing. They boil water and exhaust steam. A kettle just lets the steam go; the steam locomotive uses the steam to move.

The two of them share a key ingredient. Water. Without water neither a kettle nor a steam locomotive would serve any purpose.

Their other key ingredient is where the two differ. A kettle relies on electricity to boil its water whilst a steam locomotive requires coal.

Let's update our sentence...

A steam locomotive is a large kettle on wheels. It's made up of lots of different parts and has two main ingredients. Water and coal.

We now have the two main ingredients for our steam locomotive to work. But where was it all stored? This is where the Tender comes into its own.

The Tender is like a trailer on a car. It's the bit you can see behind the bigger locomotives. If you happen to see a locomotive without a Tender, it could mean that it has been robbed. But, perhaps more likely, it probably means you're looking at a tank engine.

Tank engines are much smaller and would mostly pull carriages on smaller railway tracks and in the shunting yards. This meant they didn't need as much coal and water as the bigger locomotives which did the longer journeys.

The Tender is split horizontally in half. The top half is reserved for coal. Some of the biggest locomotives carried 10 tonnes of coal in the Tender.

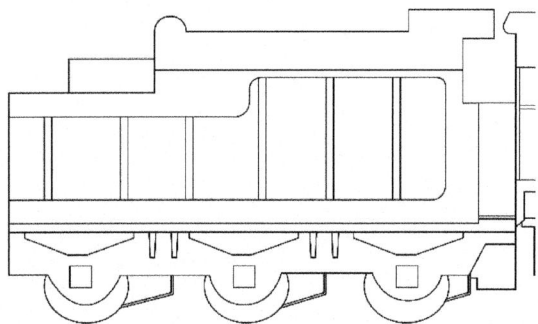

The bottom half is for water. Water is possibly the most important ingredient for a steam locomotive.

Water to a steam locomotive is like Mickey Mouse to Minnie Mouse, trumps to laughter, Marmite to toast, sprouts to my belly, bogies to noses, poo to toilets – Sorry I got carried away.

Water is really important to a steam locomotive.

Without water there wouldn't be any steam and if there's no steam then a steam locomotive goes nowhere. But all joking aside- if a steam locomotive ran out of water whilst the locomotive was hot there is a really big chance it would explode.

Between 2 and 4 thousand gallons of water could be stored in the Tender. Four thousand gallons is enough to fill sixty average sized bathtubs.

Sorry to move away from steam locomotives, but I don't know how big an average bathtub is. All I really know is that I've never been

in a bath I can fit comfortably in. I'm 6ft 4" so I don't fit in anything comfortably really. I challenge you to find out how big an average bathtub is and let me know as you're leaving your review for the book.

Anyway. Count the number of baths you have from now on and when you get to 60 you've used a Tender's worth of water.

Four thousand gallons of water sounds like a lot but in reality, it would disappear really quickly. But why did water disappear so quickly? My joke answer is that they hadn't invented plugs yet. The correct answer is that steam locomotives were thirsty beasts.

So thirsty that four thousand gallons would be gone in a few short hours. All hours, of course, are the same length- but saying a few short hours sounds more dramatic- if it bothers you then you can rewrite the sentence to say "a few regular length hours". Your call.

I think it's time for an explanation update.

A steam locomotive is a large kettle on wheels. It's made up of lots of different parts and has two main ingredients, water and coal. The water and coal is stored at the back of the locomotive in what is called the tender.

Do you think the coal and water remained in the Tender for the whole journey? If you said yes, then you're in for a surprise!

In front of the Tender is the cab. Inside the cab is the footplate. And on the footplate is where the driver and fireman work.

If you've seen a steam locomotive before you will already know cabs have a roof to keep the crew protected from inclement weather. -Rain, snow, bogies etc.

Believe it or not cabs didn't always have roofs. On early steam locomotives cabs didn't even have sides. And seats weren't really introduced until the mid-1800s. Early railway companies were afraid that their crews wouldn't work hard enough or even fall asleep if they were too comfortable. I'm fairly confident that even the heaviest of sleepers wouldn't have been able to sleep in the cab of a steam locomotive.

7 reasons why you shouldn't take a nap in a steam locomotive cab!

1) **The noise!** Controls are hissing, coal in the Tender is wobbling, the wheels make the annoying clickety clack sound and there's a lot of clanging metal.
2) **The heat!** It's really hot, the fire reached a sweaty 1500 degrees!
3) **The weather!** Rain will make it feel like you're taking a nap in the shower (please don't do that)
4) **Bumpy ride!** Imagine a bouncy castle made out of wood and metal that always has that annoying kid who never stops bouncing inside it.
5) **Falling off the engine!** I already mentioned that early locomotives didn't have sides on the cabs. It wouldn't take much for you to fall out. Not only would it be incredibly embarrassing I'm sure it would hurt as well.
6) **Accidently being thrown in the fire!** I already said the fire can be 1500 degrees- even people who like hot showers wouldn't like being thrown in the fire.
7) **Bird poo danger!** Granted this is a danger whenever we step outside but image being asleep with your mouth open when a bird poops overhead. And you thought your regular morning breathe was gross.

So, what exactly is it that the driver and fireman do?

The driver is in charge of three main controls.
1) The regulator
2) The reverser

3) The brakes

I'll write them again so we can all understand them.

1) The accelerator
2) Pretty much gears
3) The brakes

In fact, let's make it even simpler.

1) The thing that makes you go faster.
2) Decides if you'll move forward or backwards.
3) The brakes.

The fireman's main job is to shovel coal into the firebox. I bet you can't guess what's inside the firebox. I'll be honest, it took me five years to work it out.

Fire is inside the firebox.

In order to keep the fire going the fireman would have to shovel pretty much non-stop. Rather them than me I say!

Whoop whoop- explanation update time.

A steam locomotive is a large kettle on wheels. It is made up of lots of different parts and has two main ingredients, water and coal. The coal and water are stored at the back of the locomotive in what is called the tender. In the cab, the driver controls the locomotive whilst the fireman shovels coal into the firebox.

But why does a steam locomotive need a fire in the first place? It's obvious, isn't it? To make the best marshmallows in the world.

I mean, to make hot hair -air!

The fire makes hot air which travels through long tubes in the boiler where the water is. It then pops out the chimney like an invisible, and far less interesting, jack-in-the-box. As the hot air travels through the boiler, it boils the water like a giant kettle- I did tell you at the start of this section that steam locomotives were like kettles.

I know it's not been very long but let's update our explanation again. I just like putting things in bold- makes me feel important.

A steam locomotive is a large kettle on wheels. It is made up of lots of different parts and has two main ingredients, water and coal. The coal and water are stored at the back of the locomotive in what is called the tender. In the cab, the driver controls the locomotive whilst the fireman shovels coal into the firebox. The fire makes hot air which travels through long tubes in the boiler. The water around the pipes boils into steam.

Ho- Ho! Merry... hang on, I'm not Father Christmas...

So, we now have steam which is good as we're explaining how a steam locomotive works.

The steam rises to the top of the boiler and gives the driver a reading of steam pressure. Steam pressure is a steam locomotives best friend but can also be its worst enemy. Not enough steam pressure and you don't go anywhere, but too much steam pressure and the locomotive could explode. There's a dial back in the cab which measures how much steam pressure there is.

Boiler explosions were more common than a lot of people realise. And they were certainly incredibly dangerous with the potential to cause untold damage. If a boiler exploded several hundred flaming hot bolts would fire out like bullets in every direction.

Jon Cree was hired to drive the steam locomotives on the newly opened Stockton and Darlington railway. When he was refilling the locomotive *Locomotion No1* up with water he made the decision to tie down the safety valve.

Safety valves were installed in the boiler and originally used weights. When the steam pressure got too powerful the steam would lift up the weights which would make the valve open and get rid of the steam pressure.

John Cree thought his experience would mean he knew, by listening to the boiling water, when he had enough steam pressure and there would be no danger of the locomotive gaining too much– I bet he didn't believe in instruction manuals either. Because this is the unromantic railways you have probably already guessed he wasn't as good at judging boiling water as he thought he was.

On hearing the hissing of impending doom from the boiler Cree made a desperate attempt to untie the safety valve to release the pressure but to no avail. The boiler of Locomotion No1 exploded. Cree survived for two more days but did pay the ultimate price for his mistake when he died.

Locomotion No1 was rebuilt after this incident and ended up running until 1841.

After that pleasant story let's get back to how a steam locomotive works.

The steam rises upwards into the steam dome. The steam dome is the large lump that looks like a dome on top of the locomotive's boiler. Once the pressure has built up, the regulator (the locomotives accelerator) comes into play.

When the driver moves the regulator, it lets steam from the steam dome into a pipe imaginatively named the main steam pipe.

This pipe snakes down through the locomotive and into the cylinders. The cylinders are the metal box looking things near the locomotive's front wheels. These front wheels are called bogies– no word of a lie.

The steam pushes the pistons forward and backwards and the pistons moving forward and backwards is what makes the wheels turn around.

When the piston has moved forward and backwards the wheels will have spun around once. There are at least two pistons on a steam locomotive. One on each side and occasionally one in the centre.

Once the steam has pushed the piston it's allowed to drift upwards through another pipe and out of the chimney. Let's take a look at our final explanation of how a steam locomotive works.

A steam locomotive is a large kettle on wheels. It is made up of lots of different parts and has two main ingredients, water and coal. The coal and water are stored at the back of the locomotive in what is called the tender. In the cab, the driver controls the locomotive whilst the fireman shovels coal into the firebox. The fire makes hot air which travels through long tubes in the boiler. The water around the pipes boils into steam.

The steam rises to the top of the boiler and gathers in the steam dome. The driver opens the regulator which allows the steam to travel through the main steam pipe and into the pistons. The steam pushes the piston forward and backwards to move the wheels around. Once the steam has pushed the piston it travels back up through the locomotive and out of the chimney.

And that... is how a steam locomotive works. You see how simple it is when you get rid of all the complicated words? I hereby declare that from this point forward no complicated words shall ever be used again!

You've learnt a lot in this chapter so go and take a break and get yourself a banana or something.

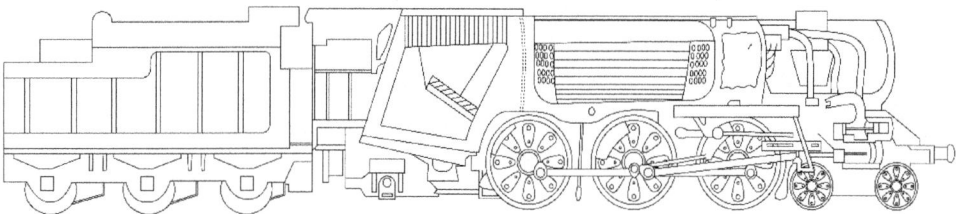

Jobs

It probably won't come as a surprise that the railways were filled with a huge variety of jobs. The railways were one of the biggest employers in history. From drivers and fireman to signalman and cleaners, the railways had it all.

In this chapter we're going to look at just a handful of the jobs on the Victorian railways.

Cleaner

It would all start as a cleaner. If you thought your parents telling you to tidy your room was bad, being a cleaner on the railways was at least four hundred million times worse – depending how messy your bedroom is of course.

The cleaner's job was obviously to clean. They'd clean locomotives, carriages, stations, underpants, toilets, dogs, pretty much everything. I'm sure you're all thinking cleaning the toilet would be the worst job they'd encounter. I will tell you now that cleaning the toilet would be a luxury compared to cleaning the locomotives themselves.

Cleaners were often teenagers, some as young as fourteen. On the surface this may seem surprising, but child labour was the norm in Victorian Britain. Nobody blinked twice when sending kids aged ten or younger into the mines or up a chimney.

New cleaner job list

1) Clean the firebox of the locomotive. This means you will have to crawl inside the firebox –after the fire has been put out– and shovel out any coal left in it. This will be done without a torch (because they haven't been invented yet). Once that's been done you need to sweep the sides to make sure the firebox is clean. Be warned, the firebox will still be quite warm when you go inside. Also be warned other workers might lock you in as a "joke".

2) Go down into the inspection pit -a hole between the rails allowing workers to walk underneath the engine- and clean out the ash pan. The ash pan catches the small debris -made up of ash and small bits of coal- which falls out of the bottom of the Firebox. Because the debris can be extremely hot still it is suggested you soak it in water first. This will make the debris into a disgusting mixture which it will be your job to clean up.

Cleaners were badly paid forcing some of them to have to sleep in the carriages. If they were discovered by the management they'd be in lots of trouble.

So, the next time you get asked to tidy your room, remember it could be worse. You could be having to clean a steam locomotive instead.

Fireman

At the age of 17 or 18 you could be promoted to a fireman. If you were to think of a fireman, you'd probably think of someone who puts out fires and drives in a red engine. A fireman on a steam locomotive was the complete opposite. Instead of putting out fires, they kept fires going.

The fireman was the muscle behind the steam locomotives power. They were tasked with shovelling coal from the tender into the firebox. The whole floor would be shaking and bouncing to make their job slightly more interesting.

They'd have to shovel one tonne of coal every single hour. That's the same weight as a polar bear or 1 million Smarties.

Driver

Being a steam locomotive driver was probably the most sought-after job on the railways. They were the Victorian version of celebrities. But becoming a driver took a lot more time, patience, and work than a lot of people realise.

You'd start as a cleaner, then be promoted to fireman on a tank engine. You'd then work your way up until you were shovelling coal on the biggest locomotives of the age.

Once you'd reached the pinnacle of fireman life you'd be promoted to a passed fireman which meant you could drive the steam locomotives inside the workshops, sheds, and shunting yards. Then you'd drive a tank engine and slowly work your way up to the big leagues.

This meant by the time you got to drive the biggest and fastest locomotives you might have worked on the railways for forty or more years. You might be wondering why it took so long? Working your way up through the ranks was like an apprenticeship and you learnt on the job. Hopefully after forty years you'd know exactly how to drive a steam locomotive- you were certainly in the wrong career if you didn't.

Guard

The guard's job on the Victorian railways was almost exactly the same as a guard's job nowadays. Their main responsibilities would have been checking tickets, which wouldn't have been easy on carriages without corridors. They were also in charge of the safety of the passengers.

The guard was based in the guard's van which was usually the last carriage of the train. These vans contained a brake to help the train stop. The early brakes on the railways were worse than rubbish, so by putting a brake at the back it helped bring the train to a stop sooner. The driver would blow the whistle to indicate for the guard to put the brake on.

Being a guard wasn't a safe career however as Thomas Port proved in 1838. Back then, the guard still sat on the roof of the carriage and as part of his duties he needed to climb onto the carriage walking boards (a piece of wood which ran underneath the doors on the side of the carriage) once the train had set off.

On the 7th of August 1838 Port went about his job like normal. He carefully climbed down from the roof of the carriage and onto the boards to check tickets through the windows and make sure no sneaky second-class passengers were sitting in first class.

As he attempted to step from one carriage to the next his foot slipped, and he tumbled down onto the track. His legs fell underneath the wheels and were crushed. -I won't get too graphic, but some body parts were hanging off as well.

Despite having both his legs chopped off by doctors Thomas Port sadly died of blood loss, three hours after the accident. I'm sure guards across the country breathed a sigh of relief when corridors were put into carriages meaning they could check tickets from the inside.

Station Master

The Station Master is exactly what you might think. Master of the station. They were in charge of the day-to-day running of the station, all the delightful health and safety and management of the station staff. They often got a house on the station grounds, and some were even known to have been gifted a horse. I once got a free pen for working somewhere- I've never been given a horse though.

Signalman

Signals are the traffic light system of the railways. Imagine a road network without traffic lights... Hopefully you're imagining absolute chaos.

The railways in this country have been split into lots of smaller sections. The rule is that only one train is allowed in one section at the same time to avoid crashes. This means that the signals are of vital importance to stop trains in the right places.

It was no different in Victorian Britain, the only difference is that nowadays the signals are controlled by a complex computer system. Back in Victorian times all the signals were manual.

I'm sure when you imagine a signal box most of you will be imagining a wooden cabin on the side of the railway track with lots of levers. If that is what you're imagining then you already have a pretty good idea of what a signal box would have looked like.

Being a signalman was a difficult job, one you had to concentrate for long hours at a time. One story is close to home (well my home- York).

There was a signalman called James Holmes. (No relation to Sherlock). He stayed awake with his very ill child and despite searching for a doctor, his child sadly died. He asked his bosses for the night off. His bosses refused. So, he trudged his way to his signal box in Thirsk. Through a mixture of sadness and tiredness Holmes fell asleep.

An express (fast) train crashed into the back of a goods train because Holmes was sleeping when he needed to change the signals. There was 8 deaths and 39 injuries.

Holmes was found guilty of manslaughter, but thanks to a kind-hearted judge he was set free. The judge had felt understandably sorry for the signalman's situation. Let's be honest, the bosses are truly the ones to blame here.

The only slight silver lining was that the signalman hours were reduced after this tragic event.

In fairness even when the signalman were doing the job to the letter some drivers chose to ignore them. A driver decided he knew better than the signals on the 16th of June 1900 when he kept going through two danger signals and collided with a local train in Slough. He was responsible for 5 deaths, 35 serious injuries and 90 complaints of whiplash.

I've just decided I'm going to start ignoring the red lights on the road so watch out everyone when I'm driving near you.

Navvy

The railway navvies were the true powerhouse behind the railways. If a tunnel needed digging, in came navvies. If you needed track placing, in came navvies. If a bridge needed building, in came navvies. If you needed a sandwich, in came navies.

You get the idea? Anything considered manual labour was done by a navvy. A navvy could shift up to 20 tonnes (about the weight of 5 elephants or 12,800 bricks) of dirt every single day. That's an insane amount and I can guarantee you'd have no chance of beating a navvy in an arm wrestle.

The name navvy came from the navigators who built to canals in the 18th century and there are lots of suggestions they were paid mostly in beer –I'd consider being paid in LEGO instead of money.

Navvies travelled around the country following railway construction. It's popular advice to "follow the money". They took massive risks and cut corners to get the work done quicker. At no point in history has it ever worked out when someone has cut a corner. Many navvies sadly died because of their own neglect of safety. Nobody cared though because it wasn't the employer's responsibility to keep their workers safe.

When it came to track placing the navvies played a massive role as well. Nowadays there are machines which lay the track for the workers, but these machines hadn't been invented in Victorian times. Track placing relied on good old manual labour.

Small sections of track would be pre-made in the factories, transported to the place they were needed and then hundreds of workers would lift them down off the transport and place them in the proper place. Talk about back breaking work.

Which job would you have liked on the railways? Personally, I would have liked to have been a mattress tester.

The fireman's shovel

Yes! Yes, you are reading this chapter title correctly. This chapter is all about the fireman's shovel.

What a strange subject for a chapter you say? I have a sneaky feeling this chapter will be my favourite in the entire book. It's not too long and waffly, it's not filled with outrageously or outlandishly big words (except those two) and it contains one of my favourite things to talk about. Poo.

Let's quickly remind ourselves what the fireman's job was, it feels like a long time ago since we spoke about the fireman and I'm sure we've all slept since then.

The fireman was the person who shovelled the coal from the back of the locomotive -the tender- and put it into the firebox to keep the fire going. Don't forget they'd have to shovel one tonne of coal an hour. 1 tonne = 1 million smarties.

If the fireman didn't shovel the coal, then there wouldn't be a fire, without the fire there wouldn't be any steam and without steam all you have is a really hard to access swimming pool.

Anyway, you're here for the unromantic stuff. Let's get back to the shovel.

The fireman's shovel has three main uses. We already know the first. Shovelling coal. Yawn- boring! I almost fell asleep writing that again, I can only apologise for your droopy eyelids.

For the second use of the fireman's shovel, I need you to close your eyes. No wait! Hang on, that's a bad idea. Go and get someone to read this next section to you so you can close your eyes. Or you can just keep your eyes open- whatever works best for you. Perhaps I should type with my eyes closed?

What's the best breakfast you can imagine? Eggs? Sprouts? Porridge? Avocado? Bogies? Toast? Pizza? Cereal? See where I'm going with this?

The second use of the fireman's shovel was using it as a

frying pan to cook a fried breakfast on. Sausage, eggs, and bacon.

Remember the firebox can reach temperatures of 1500 degrees Celsius so it could cook food in no time at all. It even comes with a sprinkle of coal dust- free of charge.

You could actually cook a lot of food on a steam locomotive. The crew would cook potatoes behind the hot pipes on the footplate, cook beans in a billy can on the shelf above the firebox, cook chicken in the smokebox -the bit behind what looks like the clock face at the front of the locomotive. The only food you'd struggle with on a steam locomotive was ice cream- unless you were incredibly quick at eating it.

But what could the third use of the fireman's shovel be? I'll tell you now, it's my favourite railway fact ever.

The third use of the fireman's shovel was...

TO POO ON!

Don't believe me? Have you ever seen a toilet on a steam locomotive? There were occasionally toilets in the carriages but never on the locomotives themselves.

If the crew needed a wee, they'd quite often just go out the side of the locomotive. That's why it wouldn't be the best idea to have a window open on your carriage. It would be even worse if it was a windy day. Can you imagine looking out the window at the same time one of the crew was having a wee? What if you had your mouth open?

But when the crew needed a poo, they went on the shovel. I mean you wouldn't want to look out your window and see the crew's bare bottoms. Though seeing their bare bottoms would be better than the dollop of poo that would be flying towards you.

The crew pooing on the shovel may be gross but it's probably the only thing you'll remember from this book. And the one thing you'll be repeating to your friends over and over again.

I want to live in a world where everyone knows this fact. You can help actually!

It's now your mission to tell everyone you know that the crew of a steam locomotive used to poo on the shovel. Together we will make it the most commonly known fact in the world!

Once the crew had finished their business, they'd throw the poo into the fire, splash some water on the shovel then place it briefly in the firebox. The heat of the fire burnt any germs to a crisp (not an actual crisp) and it was ready for more breakfast cooking.

Because I never want this chapter to end, I'm going to give you a bonus fact about the fireman's shovel – It was also a chosen weapon for a few reported murders.

One such murder happened when a fireman smacked the locomotive driver around the back of the head with his shovel. The fireman then panicked at what he'd done. He slammed on the brakes and jumped out of the cab into a swamp below.

Once the train had stopped the guard came from the back of the train and into the cab to find the fireman missing and driver dead, probably with a shovel shaped dent in his head.

A few hours later the fireman arrived at the nearest town without any trousers on, along with a suspicious brown stain on his bottom. The fireman would have regretted wearing white underpants that day.

The fireman went to the police station to explain that he hadn't pooed himself but in fact fallen out the side of the locomotive and had had to take off his trousers to escape the swamp.

The police searched the swamp and found the fireman's trousers which were covered in the driver's blood. The fireman was arrested for murder. Some suggest he was known as Poop Pants for the rest of his life. Even to this day, it's the strangest game of Cluedo anyone has ever played.

The moral of this story is don't hit anyone with a shovel. Or with anything actually. Don't hit anyone. But the bigger lesson is that you should never wear white underwear if you're going to jump into a swamp.

So, to summarise this chapter, you'll be able to tell that the fireman's shovel was a multifunctional tool. Not only was it used for shovelling coal but as a toilet, a frying pan, a murder weapon, an elaborate back scratcher, a bogie flicker and so much more.

I told you this was going to be a great chapter.

Where does the poo go?

If this was a YouTube video, then this would definitely be clickbait. What do you call the book version of clickbait? Page turn bait? Be honest, how many of you have skipped here after reading this chapter title in the contents page?

Fear not! I will of course be talking about where poo goes (I don't mean the sewers) but this chapter is all about what it was like to travel on the train.

The short version of this chapter is that travelling by rail, particularly third class, was not a pleasant experience. I will, however, go into slightly more detail.

The railways were original split into two different classes.

First and third.

The system mirrored what was already in place on the ships. First class was for the wealthy and third class was for the poor. But, because of high prices, anyone poor would have struggled to travel by rail.

Second class was introduced a little further down the line. Railway companies stated that they provided more services than the ferry companies did.

The first railway carriages were made of wood, so if there was a crash, they didn't stand much of a chance of protecting the passengers inside. In order to better protect the first-class passengers from potential crashes they placed third class on each end. They made a first-class sandwich if you like. First class in the middle and third class being the bread on either side.

This meant that if there was a crash the third-class people acted like a crumple zone for the first-class passengers. A crumple zone is where part of a vehicle, mostly car bonnets, are designed to squash together in a crash to absorb some of the force of a crash. It's the same system except the Victorian railway carriage designers used poor people instead of a bonnet.

To add insult to injury, third class passengers also had to sit over the wheels which made their ride so much bumpier.

When Rocket was pulling passengers on the Liverpool to Manchester railway, third class would have been a cramped wooden box with no roof, no seats and sides which barely counted as walls.

You'd have to stand shoulder to shoulder with numerous other people. If it was raining, you'd get wet and on a hot and sunny day you'd suffer from heat stroke.

If you were extremely lucky, you'd have a small hole drilled into the bottom of the carriage to let the rainwater drain out. If you weren't lucky then you'd get wet feet.

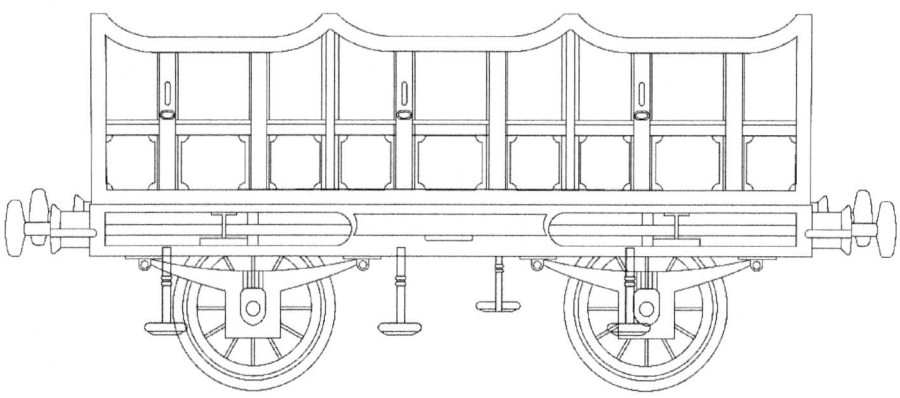

What was cool back then was that they sometimes had a carriage at the front with a live band inside to entertain the passengers. I would actually love to have live bands in place on the railways today as well.

It can't be any worse than the ignorant people who think they can play their music at top volume for the whole carriage to hear. If you're one of the people who play your music without using headphones on public transport – then I don't like you.

Whilst we're talking about things that would be cool to have on the railway. You may have seen a flipbook before. If you haven't it's the little books they draw a character on and when you move go through the pages really quickly the character dances.

Well, my idea would be to draw these characters on the side of the railway track. So, when you're travelling and feeling a little bit bored you can just look out your window and watch a little character dancing or picking its nose- scratching its bum? How cool would that be?

I'm wasted writing books- I should be out changing the world with my genius inventions...

What were we talking about? Ah yes- carriages.

Carriage development was extremely quick thanks to the high number of railway companies in the country. The company with more comfortable and more affordable would get more bums on seats than other less comfortable companies.

Competition led to carriages very quickly changing from being nothing more than wooden boxes with a small hole to drain out the rainwater to things we'd recognise as carriages today. They would still be destroyed like a hammer hitting glass if there was a crash but at least they were getting more comfortable- for first class at least.

There was still a massive issue though. The railways were too expensive. Greedy shareholders were desperate to see a return on their investment, so railway companies charged premium prices to travel.

The government finally stepped in to control the ticket prices of the railway. They needed the third-class workers to be able to travel around the country so they could work in the factories which were springing up everywhere. The railways were the fastest way to get the poor to where they needed to be. It was a common occurrence when it came to the railways for the government to only step in when it benefitted them in some way, or because something catastrophic had happened.

By being able to move factory workers around the country quicker it meant the factories could help the country make more money.

Parliament trains were introduced in 1844. It forced the railway companies to run at least one affordable train every day.

The railway companies didn't like this as it meant they didn't make as much money, so they ran this single service at awkward times in the day.

Railway companies were also afraid that the passengers who would normally travel in second class would choose to travel in the cheap carriages to save money if they were made too regularly available.

Wait... where did second class suddenly come from? Let's rewind just a little bit.

Second class was introduced as a middle class on the railways who decided they offered lots of services for passengers. Second class was somewhere between first and third class. They weren't rich but they weren't poor either. Second class would be more expensive than third class and the difference would be that there would less people squashed into your compartment. That was pretty much the only difference.

Back to the story of cheap trains.

Even with the introduction of some cheaper trains, third class passengers still struggled to pay the fair. You have to remember that some Victorian jobs paid less than a penny each week. They went to great lengths to avoid having to buy a ticket.

A guide to fare dodging, Victorian style

- Hide your baby or small child in the luggage racks above the seats. Hide them under your thickest coat so they can't be seen when the guard comes to check the tickets. Pray your child doesn't cry during the guard's visit, otherwise you could be fined for fare dodging.
- The ticket "borrower" - the rich folk carry their tickets in their top hats so they don't lose them on the journey. Sit down next to the gentleman with a ticket in their hat, yawn loudly and reach your arm across them and gently remove the ticket.

- Carrier pigeons- Get together with your friends and split the cost to buy a first-class ticket. The first of your friends will take the train to London (or wherever you're going) then tie the ticket to the leg of a carrier pigeon. The pigeon will fly the ticket back home where the next person will use the same ticket to travel the same journey. Repeat this process until the whole group have reached your destination. Please note this is only possible until the railway companies start stamping tickets. Imagine how tired the pigeon would have been!
- Push the guard off the railing when he comes to check your tickets.
- Become an expert at camouflage and make yourself blend into the seat or better still cut a hole in the back of the seat and hide yourself inside.
- Hide underneath the seats
- Pretend you don't speak English
- Ignore the guard when he comes to check tickets
- Pretend to be a statue
- Pretend to be asleep

By the 1880's second class was gotten rid of. To clarify, the second-class compartments were got rid of, not the entire second-class population of Britain.

You may wonder why they still called it third class even though there were only two classes on the railways. The reasons simple really. If a third-class passenger could travel in second class, they might get a bit big-headed and start strutting about like they're second-class citizens. How 'ruddy dare they. By keeping it known as third class it made sure the poor knew what social status was.

The average capacity for a first-class compartment was six people. There would be six individual seats that were stuffed with horsehair so would be scratchy in the summer but comfortable enough. The bottom of the first-class seats were wider and longer than seats you find today as the Victorians had extremely big bottoms.

Well, some of them would have had big bottoms but the larger seats were to accommodate the large first-class lady dresses which had a wire net making them much wider at the bottom. A crinoline is the technical term for it I believe.

Because of these big dresses the railway companies attached some handles to the sides of the doors so that the first-class passengers could use to carefully step out of the carriage without losing their balance. It wouldn't do to fall flat on your face in front of the poor people.

I've just realised that I've been writing "big dresses". I'm not sure this is the best way to write it. Is everyone thinking that the dresses travelled on their own? For full clarification people wore the dresses.

I should have mentioned it earlier but not everywhere the trains stopped had platforms, so sometimes you'd see a first-class lady having to clamber up the side of the carriage to get in – or out. It would not do for your reputation to fall in front of the commoners.

First-class passengers were even given access to a luggage compartment where they could store their big suitcases and hat boxes. Travelling in first class was pure luxury. The luggage compartment wasn't very flashy and tended just to be a bit like a storage cupboard at your home but definitely better than having your suitcase on your knee.

You found family groups would travel in the first-class compartments. Unfortunately for kids though it would normally only be the grownups of the family who travelled in first class. They'd send the kids in third class with the nanny. That's parental love for you.

Rich people were often looking for ways to save money so they could stay rich. One of their money saving tactics was to travel in second or third class. The tickets were cheaper, so they saved money. If your boss saw you in anything but a first-class compartment, they'd reduce your wage stating, "if you want to be a second-class citizen, I'll pay you like one."

I always get the impression that Victorians were really mean. I'm sure there were some nice people around- but reducing someone's pay because they didn't travel in first-class seems a little on the mean side.

The average capacity for a third-class compartment was ten people. That's twelve grownups by the way. Twelve fully-grown grownups in one compartment. What's worse is that you couldn't really open the window as the sparks and ash from the locomotive up front might enter the compartment and burn something or you'd all be choked by steam, and we already know about the risk of getting peed on!

The third-class compartment would consist of two rows of seats, both facing each other. There were no armrests so it would be more accurate to describe them as two benches. On some railway companies they would be cushioned and on others they might just be wooden. What was the same for all railway carriages, however, was the severe lack of leg room- you'd constantly be bumping knees with the person opposite.

It would get extremely stuffy inside the compartment, and a whole lot worse if someone trumped or went to the toilet for a number two. In such a small compartment everyone would know who was to blame for the smell.

Because of the cramped conditions many children, and some daredevil adults, would actually sit in the luggage racks above the seating.

*

Crime started to grow on the railways as well. There were attacks and muggings, thankfully no murders (not yet at least). Female only carriages were introduced on some railways to try and protect female travellers.

It wasn't uncommon for women to have to travel with drawing pins in their mouths. This meant if anyone tried to kiss them, they would be stabbed with the pin and back off. There was a few women who decided it would be clever to blackmail other passengers though. Some would climb into a carriage filled with men, tell them all to give her money or she would tell the train guard they all tried to kiss her. Fearing the train guard, or worse the police, would believe her the men paid up.

In 1875 Rebecca Kate Dickenson ended up clinging to the outside of a carriage to escape Colonel Valentine Baker who had made unwanted advances towards her. Baker was fined and imprisoned for a year.

*

Travelling by rail also bought up some surprises and stories you'd never expect.

There was a rich first-class male passenger travelling on his usual train when a poor looking woman and her baby got into a first-class carriage and travelled for a while. From the state of her clothes, he wasn't sure how she had afforded a first-class ticket but trying to be a polite Brit he decided not to say anything.

She kept making eye contact with the man who smiled, and she smiled back. Love was in the air? When they arrived at a station, she asked the man to watch her baby for a few moments whilst she bought a sandwich from the station. The man agreed and the woman departed, leaving her baby behind.

The woman never returned. The train set off and the man was left in charge of the child who he ended adopting. This was almost certainly the mothers plan all along She was probably so poor she couldn't afford to care for her child so took a chance on a kind stranger to give her baby a chance of a better life.

*

I know I mentioned that the carriages would get stuffy but even the warmest places get cold in the winter. In the sub-zero temperatures, travelling in a carriage would have been a frosty experience. They didn't have double glazing, so the railways came up with an idea that would not only help passengers but also make them money.

They started to rent out the Victorian version of a hot water bottle. The main difference between the Victorian and modern ones is that the Victorian hot water bottle was basically a metal tube. A first-class passenger could rent one for their journey and a porter would carry it to their compartment and place it underneath their seat.

As time moved forward the railways even started to take influence from the Romans and installed underfloor heating. They'd use steam from the locomotive and send it through a long pipe underneath the floor of the carriages. The passengers could turn a handle and steam would heat up the carriage from the floor upwards.

The majority of drivers and fireman disliked the steam heating as when it was used it meant more work for them. To be more specific it meant more work for the fireman who'd have to shovel more coal. For this reason, steam heating wasn't a feature that worked very often.

Well, I think I've dragged you along without talking about poo for long enough. The chapter is called "where does the poo go" and I can tell you that any poo a passenger did on the toilet inside carriages went all over the track. There was a hole underneath the toilet and when they were flushed everything slopped onto the ground,

Some of the Victorian pranksters would purposely fill up a toilet before flushing it. They'd then wait until they saw workers on the tracks and flush their filled loo. This would cause a lot of splash back on the track and soak the railway workers in human waste. - That's gross with a capital G.

Would you like to travel on the Victorian railways now you know a little bit more about it? It's a big no from me.

The fussy Queen

It wasn't long until the royal family joined the railway excitement though Queen Victoria herself was especially reluctant. It has absolutely nothing to do with the railways, but I recently found out that Victoria wasn't actually her first name. Victoria was her second name.

Her first name was Alexandrina. Queen Alexandrina doesn't roll off the tongue quite as well as Queen Victoria. I wonder what the Victorian era would have been called if she'd preferred to go by her first name? I'd put my vote to "the Alexandrina dynasty". Now I've read that a few times I think it actually sounds pretty cool, let's hope there's a parallel world out there where the Alexandrina dynasty is a real thing.

All joking aside, I'd like to place on record my thanks to Queen Victoria for not using her first name. I struggle to pronounce most names, but I'd stand no chance of pronouncing Alexandrina every time I wanted to talk about her- it's hard enough to type it.

The first member of the royal family to travel on the railways was a lady called Queen Adelaide in 1840. Don't panic if you haven't heard of her- I hadn't heard of her either. Queen Adelaide was Queen Victoria's Aunt and had been the wife of William IV (4th) until he had passed away.

From the accounts I've found Adelaide was a pretty awesome lady. She gave a lot of money to charities, was always nice to the future Queen Victoria, had the Australia city named after her and oddly was seriously ill a few months before her husband, the king, passed away in 1837. She recovered from her illness, obviously, unless it was a ghost travelling on her carriage in 1840.

Adelaide had her very own carriage built so she could travel from London to Birmingham. It was pretty much a road carriage which would have been pulled by horses placed on a railway chassis. One cool addition they made to the carriage was to let the back of a seat to lift up so Adalaide could place her feet in the now lifted seat, which led into a black box on the end of the carriage to lie down and rest her weary eyes.

Back in the 1800's the roads were far below modern standards. They were unclean, unsafe, and uncomfortable. If you think we have a pothole problem nowadays it would have been much much worse back then. The railways offered a more comfortable way of travelling, particularly for the higher reaches of Victorian society.

At the age of 23, Queen Victoria became the first reigning monarch to travel by train on the 13th of June 1842. Her husband, Prince Albert, was the persuading force to get her on board. Victoria and Albert travelled between Paddington and Slough. (Slough was the closest station to Windsor Castle).

The Great Western Railway had only a few days' notice that Victoria wished to travel by the railway. Luckily, they'd already built her a royal carriage. Can you imagine how awkward it would have been if they hadn't?

They were nervous about crowds gathering on stations and

other places close to the railway line and with so little time to put in crowd control you can probably imagine how much sweat leaked from the railway workers on the morning of the 13th of June.

Victoria hoped the railways would be safer than travelling by horse and carriage. She'd be Queen for 5 years and had already had 4 assassination attempts on her life. That's almost 1 a year!

The locomotive used to pull Queen Victoria was called 'Phlegethon' (I challenge you to say that ten times quickly. In fact, I challenge you to say it once).

According to Greek mythology, Phlegethon is a river of lava in the underworld. I've heard some mean things said about Windsor, but I wouldn't have imagined it was the underworld.

Victoria's train was formed of 7 carriages in total with Victoria's carriage wedged in the middle to provide extra protection in case of a crash. The train was controlled by Daniel Gooch and Isambard Kingdom Brunel. (Until I spotted it, I typed Burnel instead of Brunel- not important to the book, just thought I'd share)

Victoria's coachman (the person in charge of steering the horses) insisted on travelling on the footplate during the journey. He regretted it quickly though as his beautiful scarlet uniform was completely ruined by the smoke and soot. I suppose he chose the hard way to learn that the footplate wasn't a place to wear fancy clothes. After all, drivers and fireman don't wear smart suits to work for a reason. (It would make the whole train experience more stylish though)

Victoria's journey in 1842 was much quicker than it would have been by traditional stagecoach, it shaved 2-hours off the 18-mile journey. I've spent about 3 months trying to think of a way of saying less dusty so it flowed properly- I never succeeded which is why I'm writing that her journey would have been less dusty (dustless?) on the train.

After her first railway journey there was no stopping Victoria. In a letter the next day saying she had been "quite charmed" by the experience. Companies from all over the country were desperate to make carriages for her and the royal carriages led the way in carriage design.

Because Victoria showed her acceptance of the railways to her (mostly) loyal subjects a lot of the early fear of the railways was eliminated. If it was safe enough for the Queen, it must be safe for everybody.

But you will have noticed that this chapter is called 'the fussy Queen'. There were a few rules you had to follow when Queen Victoria was travelling on the railways. She made them all up as well.

The problem is, you can't really say no to the Queen, so the crew had to follow them whether they wanted to or not.

Queen Victoria's railway travelling rulebook

1) Do NOT travel faster than 40 miles per hour during the daytime. I have a special signal on top of my carriage, and I will use it if I feel you are driving too fast.

2) Do NOT travel faster than 30 miles per hour during the night. I need my beauty sleep and will not have it disturbed by you driving like a lunatic.

3) When a toilet stop is needed, I will NOT use the toilet onboard my carriage- even though I have the first ever carriage with a toilet on. You must stop at a railway station so I can use a first-class waiting room- even though this means that the station is bought to a standstill whilst I go pee-pee. (Or poo-poo)

4) I will NOT eat whilst on the move. If I want a snack, you will stop the train. Eating on the move is bad for my digestive system and Albert doesn't like it when I have an upset stomach- my trumps become unbearably smelly. It also becomes impossible to win the game I like to play of balancing bowls full of food on my head.

5) I will NOT walk through the corridor that connects 2 carriages together, you must stop the train if I want to cross into my sleeping quarters.

6) I will NOT accept modern electricity in my carriages. My lamps will be lit how they should always be- with oil. I for one enjoy the smell.

7) The only modern technology I will graciously allow in my carriage is the little button on the wall which calls an attendant every time I push it. (I sometimes do this when I don't need anything, just to make sure it's still working- lol)

Hang on... did I just seriously write lol in a chapter about Queen Victoria? I can only apologise- let's hope the proof-readers take that out.

Some drivers lost their heads at these rules. One of them did so literally. In 1848 a driver named David Fenwick lost his head when he hit a bridge after he climbed into the Tender to try and fix the communication cord to talk to the royal carriage.

So next time someone asks you who would win a fight between a bridge and a human head- you can tell them that the bridge would win.

As I briefly mentioned earlier there was a need to keep the Queen safe when she was travelling on the railways. During her 63-year reign Victoria survived 8 assassination attempts- and they're only the ones we know about!

To minimise the risk of travelling on the train the railways introduced pilot trains. One would travel 15 minutes in front of Victoria and the other roughly 15 minutes behind her train. This meant if any scallywags with dreams of murdering the queen had blocked the line ahead or prepared an ambush the pilot train would come across it first, so they had time to stop the Queen's train and go a different way.

This sounds sensible right? But it came with some problems. If Queen Victoria decided she wanted to stop in the middle of nowhere for something to eat, it meant that two other trains had to stop as well. This meant more of the track was blocked and there was a lot more disruption to everyone else's train journeys. I bet Victoria ate slowly on purpose. (Wait- can I get my head chopped off for saying that?)

Andy's Amazingly Awesome fact

Queen Victoria wasn't a big fan of Newcastle. She'd once been charged for a meal. Not happy about her food not being free she apparently drew the curtains on her carriage every time she travelled through the city.

Queen Victoria made her final journey by rail after she passed away. Her body travelled by train (I'm guessing in a coffin) from Paddington Station to Windsor for her funeral service.

And so departed a queen who had seen so many technological firsts. She'd seen electricity, flushing toilets, sewing machines, typewriters, radios, the bike with the big wheel that I can't remember the name of- possibly ice cream, oh- and the railways were all invented during her reign. (My personal favourite is the flushing toilet)

I wonder what the first person who saw a flushing toilet would have thought. Can you remember what you thought the first time you saw a flushing toilet?

The travelling post office

I mentioned at some point in the previous pages of the book that everything was transported by rail, and mail was no different. Mail being transported by the rail was seen at the very beginning of the railways on the 11th of November 1830. On that day mail was transported on the Liverpool to Manchester railway which was only a month old at the time.

By the end of the decade railway companies were actually required to carry mail. To this end specialised carriages were developed to carry letters, parcels and if you were in America, a child.

Mail being transported by rail was great news for those who wanted their mail to be delivered quickly. The new trains were much faster than the old mail coaches which were pulled by horses.

The post being transported by rail wasn't great news for everyone- in particular the station workers. Whenever the station master announced the mail train was leaving in the early hours of the morning it meant an all-night shift for those involved. It was quite remarkable how many workers suddenly became ill when a night shift was announced. Some of the larger stations had staff purposely employed to sort the mail into the right piles so they got put on the right train. Smaller stations relied on the porters to do it all.

From 1838 onwards, some of the carriages were converted into moving sorting offices. This meant along one side of the carriage there would be a series of pigeonholes- or lots of post boxes if you prefer to think of it that way. They had staff on board who would sort mail as the train was moving. As time moved forward and the speeds of trains increased, workers might be trying to sort letters whilst moving at 60mph. I hope they didn't get travel sick when they read.

The first version of a mail sorting carriage was actually a converted horse box fitted with wooden pigeonholes. It ran from Birmingham up to Liverpool on the 20th of January 1838.

Travelling post offices were used all the way up to 2004. Scary to think how long ago that was now actually.

By sorting the mail on the move it meant that letters could be loaded into a sack and dropped off at stations on route. These carriages became known as a travelling post office.

The railway companies were forced to transport the rail by law. The Railways (Conveyance of Mails) Act of 1838 gave the postmaster-General – yep, even the royal mail had a general back then- the power to dictate when trains were going to be run to carry the mail. If a railway company refused to carry letters, they were charged a whopping £20! -Remember £20 was a lot of money back in 1838.

But how did they get the post on and off the carriages? Some were done in what I'd consider to be the normal but less exciting way. The post carriages would stop at the platforms and the bags of mail would be placed on the carriage, they'd wait for the signal to turn green, and they carry on.

The second way was certainly more adventurous and exciting, but maybe not the best method- particularly if there was anything fragile in the mail. The travelling post office would pick up and drop off mail without stopping.

I can imagine the reviews on the post office website already.

---

1 star- My delicate China bowls arrived in such a state I imagine the box was rugby tackled by a rhinoceros somewhere on route.

On the side of the carriage would be a net that could be pushed out and pulled in. Bags of mail would be hung on hooks on the side of the track and as the post train thundered passed the net would catch them. The force of hitting the bag would unhook them from their posts. The workers would then pull the bags in through a small wooden door and get to sorting. – You can see why transporting anything fragile like your finest plates or newly built LEGO structure.

The roles would be reversed when the post carriage was dropping off mail without stopping. They would hook the mail bags on a hook and as they went passed an allocated signal box or other location the bags would be caught in a net and be left behind.

You could also send letters and parcels with the guard in the guard's van. The guard would store it in his compartment before handing it over to the appropriate station officials when they got to their destination. A lot of people would have done this with postcards or sending more fragile parcels to friends, families, and enemies.

I recently learnt there are companies around nowadays that you can pay to send people envelopes full of glitter so when they open it glitter goes everywhere and they won't be able to trace it back to you. I'm not sure if the Victorians had similar services, I just wanted to share that little piece of knowledge.

The travelling post offices are just more reasons why the railways changed the face of the country. Letters which might take months to reach people on mainland Europe could now be with them in just a week. The world was changing- and quickly.

There are stories of haunted travelling post offices- rumour is when you look inside you see a ghost of a postman still sorting letters into the pigeonholes. Talk about being deadicated (get it?) to your job.

Snack break!

Hands up who has ever been sat on a train and suddenly become hungry? I don't know about yours, but my hand is high in the air which is making typing really slow because I'm only using one hand so I'm going to put it down now.

Being hungry on the train is not a 21st century thing, it has been happening since the railways began. Nowadays we would just make the perilous journey down the train corridors- plagued with people's legs and sticky out elbows- is there anything more awkward when you're trying to pass someone in the train corridor? You know one of you is ending up sitting on a stranger's knee.

Once you make it the food section of the train you buy your food, then make the dangerous journey back to your seat. Luckily, most services have a nice trolley which comes down for you to buy smaller snacks and drinks from to make our train journey less stressful.

Sadly, our Victorian counterparts didn't have it quite as lucky. The carriages didn't have corridors, so they weren't able to bring a trolley to each compartment and passengers couldn't make a tricky journey to the food compartment.

To this end stations provided a whole host of food vendors on the platforms for passengers to fill their bellies and quench their thirst. The only problem was that you had to make sure you were back on the train when it set off again as they wouldn't wait for you. Most companies would put an effective lunchbreak on their longer journeys. In these breaks the train would stop at an allocated station for a longer time to allow passengers to go to the toilet – despite most passengers probably weeing out the window- and get some refreshments.

Despite the wide range of choice, most passengers would go for soup. It was a sound strategy as any pre-made sandwiches would have been out in the open since 4 or 5 in the morning so would be nice and stale and you didn't know how "in-date" the fruit or anything was.

What they didn't know is that there was a slight issue with soup. Because the railways were filled with people who were only interested in making money, you won't be surprised to hear that nothing was different with the people who worked on the stations. Money making was the only thing that mattered.

To this end, the owners of the vendors making soup would instruct their chefs to heat up the soup much hotter than necessary. This meant that as people ate the soup, they weren't able to eat it quickly. Because they couldn't eat it quickly, they left a fair bit of soup at the bottom of the bowl.

This is where it gets a little bit disgusting. The vendor staff would swoop in and pick up the leftover soup. Now I'm sure you're thinking they thew the leftover soup away. You'd be thinking wrong. They'd take all the leftover soup, put it all in a big pan, reheat it and serve to the next unlucky customers who came along.

The very thought of it makes me feel a little bit sick. I think travelling back to Victorian Britain would make a health and safety inspector faint from shock. I'm not too surprised that the soup got reused as it was common practice for people to use tealeaves to pick up dust when they were sweeping the floors at home. They'd then give them a quick fan in the wind and sell the tea leaves to teamakers- the teamakers would them sell them back to the public to use in their drinks. I'm starting to think these Victorians were kinda gross.

Speaking of tea- how long do you brew your tea for before you take the teabag out? As a Yorkshireman I brew my tea for a shamefully little amount of time – I blame the Birmingham half of my blood for not liking ultra-strong northern tea. At any rate- the most time I've heard someone brewing their tea for is five minutes which seems an awfully long time.

If you were to buy a nice cuppa from the station in Victorian Britain at 4pm there is a good chance the tea would have been brewing for 12 hours. Tea so strong it would probably break a window if you thew it at one. I'll pay someone £10 to try a 12-hour brewed cup of tea – forget that actually! Does someone want to pay me £10 to try a 12-hour brewed cup of tea? I'm sure it tastes delightful.

Eventually the Victorians were saved from the platform vendors by the introduction of corridors and dining carriages.

Dining carriages started to pop up towards the end of the 1870s in this country and were first seen on the Great Northern railway. They quickly developed to the point where you could have a three-course meal on board and even third-class carriages were pretty decent.

The railways couldn't quite let go of the idea of just trying to make as much money as possible though, so they used to design the carriages to have uncomfortable chairs on purpose. This meant that people would eat their food and not linger to chat afterwards. This helped create a good customer turnover and keep the tills ringing.

To cater for the new dining carriages, they had kitchen sections installed as well. They put the gas supply for the cooker in the nice and safe position underneath the carriage so if it hit anything hard it could explode, and meals were prepared on board a moving train.

I wish I had a picture of just how big the frying pans were- you could easily cook 40 sausages on them, and they were crazy heavy to stop them wobbling around as the train went on its journey. They put a safety bar around the hob as well to stop any pans falling off. Most of the floors were still wooden so hot oil landing on them wouldn't be an ideal situation- I haven't found any reports of that actually happening.

If the chefs ran out of food, they had an expert way of letting the next station know. They'd write a list of ingredients they needed and put it inside a hollowed-out potato. They'd then throw the potato at the next signal box they passed.

On seeing the potato land on the ground (or being scared out of their mind by a potato breaking their window) the signalman would use the new telegraphs to send a message to the next station.

The station master would get the message and would then order the porter to have the ingredients the dining train needed taken to the platform it would be arriving at.

I proposed at my place of work we stop using e-mails and start just writing letters and placing them in potatoes. It was dramatically turned down as the bosses didn't like the idea of employees lobbing potatoes at each other – a more painful version of a snowball fight.

Now that everyone undoubtedly needs a snack– let's end this chapter here – I'm going to get some marmite and toast.

The first railway murder

On the night of the 9th of July 1864, a driver of a train thought he saw a dog on the side of the track in North London. Like every single human on the planet would do he stopped the train, delaying all the passengers, in the hope of the opportunity to pet a dog.

To the disappointment of the driver, he hadn't seen a dog on the side of the track. What he found was the badly injured and unconscious body of a seventy-year-old banker called Thomas Briggs. Briggs sadly died later in the night and will be forever known as the victim of the first railway murder.

Up the line at Hackney station people (also bankers- was it only bankers that travelled on the railways?) climbed into a first-class carriage ready for a pleasant journey home. The blood stains on their chairs soon put an end to that, and their chance of being able to wear the same trousers to work the next day. A guard inspected the carriage to confirm it was blood and not paint. Also, in the carriage they found a walking stick, a bag, and a black beaver hat.

I'm fairly confident in thinking it would have been a beaver top hat, but it could equally have been a blue hat from the beaver scouts or one of those fluffy hats you see people wear in cold climates, you know the ones with the bits that cover your ears. (I sometimes amaze myself at my amazing descriptions). Acting quickly, the guard locked the carriage door and handed over the items to the police.

Naturally there was public outcry about the murder. Never before had someone been murdered on the train. They had been luggage theft and the occasional mugging, but never a killing. People were scared, angry, and wanted to know how the railways were going to protect the passengers. No matter what industry you work in, murder is bad for business.

A reward was offered by the bank which Briggs had worked for. I've tried to find out how much was offered as a reward but most of the sources just say, "a substantial reward". I'll leave it to your imaginations how much money would have been involved.

A jeweller by the name of John Death (of all the surnames to have in this situation!) spoke to the Police about a man who had exchanged a gold chain in his shop. This gold chain was examined and was found to have belonged to the victim Thomas Briggs. But who had the man been?

A cabman was next to come forward. A young German fellow by the name of Franz Muller had been engaged to his eldest daughter and had given her a small cardboard box from Death's shop. I'm just guessing, but I'm going to presume there was something in the box. As fun as cardboard boxes are you can't build a good fort with a small one. It would be a very strange gift to give someone a cardboard box with death written on it- try it for your friend's birthday and record the reaction.

The big piece of evidence the cabman had, though, was that the beaver hat they had found on the carriage was one he had bought for Franz Muller. The young fellow had been so excited about being able to finally buy his former girlfriend a cardboard box he forgot to pick his hat back up! Either that or his fear of hat hair forced him to abandon his hat.

The cabman (I hope that was his real name) gave a picture of Muller to the Police who showed it to the jeweller who confirmed that Muller had been the man who had exchanged the gold chain. He also confirmed Muller had incredibly bad manners, but great hair.

There was a problem. Muller had sailed to New York on the 15th of July. How were they going to be able to arrest him? He had a head start. Back then it took the faster steamships just over 15 days to cross the Atlantic. Muller hadn't taken a faster steamship though so it would take him considerably longer.

Inspector Tanner and Sergeant Clarke set sail from Liverpool on the 20th of July and, despite Muller having a 5-day head start, arrived in New York on the 5th of August. Muller wouldn't arrive for another three weeks. This is where the two Police officers had been clever. They got themselves a three-week holiday paid for them.

When Muller arrived in New York they arrested him. After rooting through his pockets, they found a watch and a hat that had belonged to Thomas Briggs. Why had he felt the need to swap hats with the man he'd just killed! Was this whole thing because of hat envy?

Muller was bought back to London where he appeared in the Old Bailey at the end of October 1864. He tried to argue that the hat left in the carriage had belonged to the unnamed cabman but to no avail. He was publicly executed.

The scenes at public executions were more party like than they should have been. People got drunk and sang songs- they made it into a inappropriate event. It was for these reasons that public executions were gotten rid of four years later in 1868.

*

Sadly, the murder of Thomas Briggs wasn't the last murder on the railways. The chance of being murdered became part of the railway experience.

There were a few safety features which were added to the railways as results of murder. Corridors were added to give people a chance to run away or to move if someone smelly sat in the carriage. They also brought the emergency brake cord inside the carriage rather than on the outside (I should say it still took the train about a mile to stop). For context one mile is the same as running around the edges of a football pitch five times.

There were lots of horrific murder stories that came out of Victorian times and a fair number of them involved the railways. There were stories of people murdering someone in a location, chopping up the victim's body into small pieces, placing the pieces in a suitcase, and throwing the little parts out of the window as they travelled on the train.

There were other stories where someone would murder someone, chop up their body and put it in a suitcase and leave the case in a railway station. The station workers would think it was lost property and take it to the lost property department where it would be stored and, as they would have presumed, collected by the owner. A few weeks later, they'd start to wonder what the bad smell was.

Pretty unromantic stuff....

In 1897 Miss Elizabeth Camp became the first female to be murdered on the railways. Her body was found in a second-class carriage with a damaged skull. The murder weapon had been a pestle (the thing you use to grind spices). Police found it further up the track after an investigation. They questioned several people, but the murderer was never found.

*

The railways were even involved in the first ever arrest made with the help of technology back in 1845. Honestly these railways got themselves involved in everything.

John Tawell met Sarah Hart when he employed her as a nurse to look after his dying wife, who sadly passed away in 1838 (He also lost his eldest son in 1838 and his younger son had died five years earlier in 1833).

John and Sarah had an affair and had two children together. They never married. Tawell married a few years later and paid Sarah £1 a week in child maintenance.

In 1843 Tawell fell upon hard times and needed to reduce his outgoings. Most people would look for a second job, cancel their Netflix subscription (or use a friends or families account rather paying for their own), they might even start a blog. For reasons unknown Tawell decided that murdering Sarah Hart would be the best way forward. It would save him £1 a week if nothing else.

On the 1st of January 1845, Tawell bought some poison and went to visit Sarah in Slough. He distracted her and put the poison in her beer. Hart's neighbour heard a loud groan then saw Tawell leave the house. She dashed over to see if Hart was alright. She found her writhing on the ground, foaming at the mouth. The neighbour raised the alarm but sadly a doctor couldn't get there quick enough to save Hart's life.

Reverend E.T. Champnes was, if nothing else, a quick thinker. He got a description of what John Tawell looked like and dashed off to the railway station. He saw Tawell boarding the train but was too late to stop it from departing.

What Tawell hadn't remembered is that Slough had a new telegraph which meant messages could be sent quicker than ever before using Morse code. The telegraph had only been invented eight years earlier in 1837 by Samuel Morse- hence the name Morse code.

The station master sent a message to Paddington Station in London. He told him that a murder had just taken place, the suspect was on the 7.42pm train from Slough to London, what he was wearing and which carriage he was in.

The message was received by Sergeant William Williams.

Hang on... pause

I'm sorry but these names have to been made up for protection of something. Who calls their kid William Williams? - that's like me being called Andy Andy or worse Lickley Lickley- I might call my first-born child that actually.

William Williams was a great Sergeant though. When he was informed that the train carrying John Tawell had arrived, he put a plain coat over his uniform and went to meet the train. He saw Tawell getting out of the carriage and followed him to an omnibus.

For those not from the Victorian era an omnibus was a horse pulled carriage which people either sat inside or on the roof.

Williams sat in the conductor seat on the bus, Tawell mistook him as the conductor (easy mistake to make, I suppose), and paid him the money for the ride when he got off the bus. (To this day we don't know if Williams gave the money to the bus company, or if he stole it.)

Williams followed Tawell to his house before returning to Paddington where he visited Inspector Wiggin Wiggins (I made his first name up as I don't know what it actually was- but Wiggin Wiggins has a ring to it.) The next morning William Williams and Wiggin Wiggins (is that as hard to say as it is to write?) went off to arrest Tawell.

On finding Tawell, in a café, he protested saying he hadn't been in Slough the day before. Williams, probably fiddling with his moustache, announced that Tawell had been in Slough the day before and had paid him the sixpence fare for the omnibus when he'd gotten off the train.

I wasn't there but I imagine there were gasps that could be heard by the Queen in Buckingham Palace. At this revelation the waitress probably dropped the tray of expensive plates she was carrying, and someone definitely walked into a table. People outside would have walked into lampposts because they were so distracted and amazed by this revelation. It would have been wonderful to have been able to see John Tawell's face- I wonder if he asked for his sixpence back?

A post-mortem of the victim's body said the cause of death was poisoning by prussic acid. The lawyer of Tawell explained that prussic acid was found in apple pips (seeds) and Sarah Hart had died because she had eaten a lot of apples over the festive period.

This lawyer should never have worked again. We all know there isn't a single person who eats fruit and vegetables over the festive period.

After some research though apple seeds do release cyanide when they come into contact with the human digestive system. If you do eat apple seeds in the hope of growing an apple tree out your mouth, perhaps you should stop. Google says it's not enough to kill you but I'm not sure we should trust it.

People actually stopped buying so many apples when they heard about the lawyer's defence in court. That's one of those beautiful moments in history that I feel not enough people know about. That's also a great quiz question for you all the start using.

Q- Why did the sale of apples drop in Victorian Britain during 1845?

Because a lawyer claimed apple seeds had poisoned an innocent woman in the attempts to get a murderer off free.

Anyway, John Tawell admitted to the murder on Friday 28th of March 1845 and was hung outside the court to a crowd of 10,000 people.

So, have these murder stories made you more or less likely to travel on the railways in Victorian times? It's put me off travelling back in 1845 and trying to sell apples if nothing else.

If you happen to invent a time machine and have a great desire to travel on the Victorian railways perhaps you should make sure you can get a carriage by yourself. Or invent a forcefield to protect yourself from potential attackers before you go.

To be honest we all know the best way to stop other people getting into a carriage with us. Eat lots and lots of sprouts, topped with several tins of beans. Then let your trumps do the work for you.

The Great Gold Robbery

For our next chapter I'm going to tell you the story of the Great Gold Robbery of 1855. By the mid-1800s pretty much everything was transported by rail. Passengers, letters, parcels, gold from the banks, hats, coats, pigeon feathers, Queen Victorias bogie collection, and animals to name but a few. Speaking of animals, what do you think giraffes did when they got to a tunnel?

The aim of the gold robbery is exactly what you expect. To rob gold from a train. This particular train was travelling from London to Paris on the South-eastern Railway, which was a railway that travelled from London to Folkstone, where goods and passengers caught a ferry and travelled to France.

In the guards, van were three boxes of gold bullion, coins, and rare Pokémon cards. Okay, I made the Pokémon cards up but there really was gold bullion and coins, though you wouldn't put it past anyone robbing a train for a Charizard card.

If you've ever watched any sort of heist film in your life you will know there's always a highly skilled team which is brought together by the brains of the operation and the tale of the gold robbery of 1855 is no different. But were they really a highly skilled team? Let's meet them and find out.

The planner of the robbery was a man named William Pierce. He was 37 years old and had actually been fired by the south-eastern railway, so he clearly had some harsh feelings towards the company. Pierce was joined by a professional safe cracker called Edward Agar, who was in a lot of debt.

Like all good robberies the two of them needed a man on the inside and this particular man was James Burgess. He was a guard for the south-eastern railway and was often in charge of the trains that carried the high valued gold bullion.

Next was Fanny Kay who was Edward Agar's partner who he shared a child with. It had been Kay who had introduced Agar to Burgess a few years before the robbery. She wasn't part of the heist crew but plays an important role towards the end. She's like that big actor in a film who makes a shock cameo appearance at the end.

The robbery would require another guy on the inside, so William Tester joined the crew. Tester worked in the traffic department at London Bridge station, so he had access to all the information on what was being transported on each train.

The plan was simple. Get copies of the two keys needed to open the safes the gold was stored in, sneak aboard the train as it stopped at London Bridge station, take the gold, sneak off the train, and buy a LEGO Death Star, or whatever the Victorian equivalent of a LEGO Death Star was. (Probably a yo-yo or something).

Pierce and Agar began to stake out where the keys were located in Folkstone. They weren't too good at remaining hidden and attracted the attention of the railway police. Fearing their plan was going to be rumbled by the coppers, they made the decision that Agar would stake out the location alone. After drinking at a local pub Agar discovered that one of the keys was looked after by the superintendent and the other was locked in a cabinet in the railway offices located near Folkstone pier.

They now knew where the two keys they needed to unlock the safes were kept. But how were they going to get them? They decided William Tester was best placed to be able to do it.

When new safe keys were issued Tester was able to smuggle them out of the railway office for a short time. Tester, however, was not cool under pressure and ended up bringing two copies of the same key. I can only guess what Agar and Pierce said to him when they realised his error. We'll never know what was actually said but I'm sure "plonker" and "nitwit" were heard in the surrounding streets. Focussing on the positives though, they now had one of the two keys they needed to rob the gold. They made a copy of it and send Tester back to return the original keys.

To locate where the superintendent kept the other key, Agar used a fake name to buy a package to be delivered to Folkstone station. When he went to collect it, he watched craftily as the superintendent went and got his safe key from a cupboard.

Now he knew where the key was stored all they needed was an opportunity to borrow it without being seen. Such an opportunity arrived a week or so later when the staff members left the office to assist in a recently arrived shipment. Agar acted as lookout (they probably had a well-rehearsed whistle to warn each other that trouble was coming) as Pierce snuck into the office, opened the cupboard, and stole the key. Agar got a copy of it in wax (to later be made into a key) and Pierce returned the original key to the cupboard. The station staff were none the wiser.

The gang of soon-to-be gold robbers now had both keys they needed to open the safes. To make sure their self-made keys worked Agar travelled on the Folkestone train several times whilst their guard on the inside, James Burgess, was on duty. Burgess tested the keys in the safes so Agar could adjust them. They did this until the keys slid effortlessly into the safes and unlocked them.

The next ingredient for their gold robbing scheme was to buy about one hundred kilograms of lead shot. You use lead shot in shotguns. The gang didn't own any shotguns, the lead shot was for a different purpose (see if you can work out what they were going to use it for before you read the rest of the story).

They then bought some courier bags which were basically the Victorian version of bum (ha-ha- I wrote bum) bags or as the Americans call them "fanny packs". They also bought carpet bags like Mary Poppins which they were going to use to carry the lead shot onto the train, and the gold off the train.

The squad was ready. They called on their traffic department worker William Tester to change the staff working rosters to make sure Burgess was working on the evening trains for the month of May. They arranged for Burgess to wipe his nose with a white handkerchief if there was gold onboard a train. Their opportunity came on the 15th of May 1855 when Burgess wiped away his bogies with a white handkerchief.

Agar and Pierce purchased two first-class tickets and gave their bags to Burgess for storage in the guard's van, where the safes full of gold were. Pierce settled down for a comfortable journey in first class but, just as the train was about to department, Agar snuck into the guard's van and hid under Burgess's clothes. (I should say spare clothes that Burgess wasn't wearing, can you imagine how obvious he would have been if Agar had hidden in Burgess's coat- things like that apparently only work in cartoons).

Once the train set off, Agar was surprised to find only one of the safes actually locked. He used the single key to unlock the other and pulled out the bullion boxes which contained the gold. Just in case you were wondering a bullion box was a wooden box.

Agar carefully got the gold bars from the boxes, being careful not to break the boxes, and weighed them on a set of scales he had in his bag. Have you guessed what the lead shot was for yet? Well let me tell you. Once Agar knew how much the gold in each box weighed, he put the same weight of lead shot back in the box.

They encountered a problem when they weighed the final box as it turned out the gold weighed more than the amount of lead shot, they had left and what was worse is Agar accidently damaged the box. Agar took the gold, leaving some behind to try and make sure the box still weighed the same. There were still a couple of safes to search and Agar didn't want to use up all his lead shot too soon.

Why was Agar so careful with how much each bullion box weighed? (Also, how many times I have I written weighed in the last two paragraphs?) The protocol was to weigh the gold bullion boxes when they reached Boulogne in France, so Agar had to be careful nothing was amiss to avoid raising suspicion.

Damaging a bullion box could cause a problem further down the line (pun intended) so Agar repaired it as best he could. Hopefully he was better at DIY than I am otherwise he'd never get away with it.

Agar only had a 30-minute journey to make the transfer and try and repair the box as when the train arrived at Redhill station he had to hide again. A bag, containing some of the gold, was given to Tester who returned to the South-Eastern railway offices and made sure he was seen by some of his work colleagues so he had an alibi and couldn't be connected to the robbery if it was discovered.

Pierce joined Agar and Burgess in the guard's van, and they examined some of the other safes. One of them contained some American Gold Eagles which were ten-dollar gold coins. Surprisingly, they were worth ten dollars each and the last scraps of lead shot were used as a much less valuable replacement.

The train arrived in Folkstone. Agar and Pierce hid as the safes were removed from the guard's van. Once the safes had gone, they made their way through the train, back to their first-class carriage where they sat until the train reached Dover. Once in Dover they collected their bags, which were now filled with gold, from the guard's van and skipped merrily down the lane to a hotel, throwing all the keys and tools into the English Channel (the part of the Atlantic Ocean which separates Britain and France) as they went. The temptation to let out an evil laugh must have been almost impossible to resist.

They returned to London on the 2am train with almost 100kg of gold which would have been roughly worth £12,000 in 1855. To show how much they'd stolen that £12,000 would be worth just under £400,000 today. You can buy 666,666 (six hundred and sixty-six thousand, six hundred and sixty-six) packets of Smarties for that. I don't want to offend anyone who likes Smarties, but I think you could probably spend the money on more interesting things. The two newly rich friends arrived back in London at 5am.

Meanwhile the now lead filled boxes had arrived in Boulogne and one of the crew noticed that one of the boxes was damaged. He didn't see any reason to worry about it. The boxes were weighed and all of the boxes, apart from one, were heavier than they were supposed to be. One box weighed about 18kg less than it should. (Turns out Agar needed better scales) For some reason this didn't alarm anybody in Boulogne, so they placed the boxes on another train which transported them to Paris.

Once in Paris the boxes were weighed again, and it did raise some eyebrows there. The crew opened the boxes and must have dropped their early morning baguettes when they found the gold had been replaced with lead shot. They quickly sent a message to London. The two countries then tried to play the blame game. The British said the robbery must have taken place in France and the French said the robbery must have taken place in Britain.

If they'd stopped arguing for long enough, they may have noticed that Agar and Pierce had some American Eagles changed to British pounds at a currency exchange (or a money-changers shop as they called them back them). They received £213 pounds from the first shop then another £200 from the second one they visited.

Eventually, France and Britain agreed that the robbery had taken place in Britain, so the police rolled up their sleeves and got to work.

The finger was first pointed at James Burgess, but he was cleared of any suspicion thanks to working for the company for almost 15 years. (Does this mean to rob a bank and get away with it you just need to work at a bank for 15 years and they'll never suspect you?) William Tester had an alibi that he'd been at the South-Eastern railway office when the train was still on the way to Folkestone, so he too was cleared of any suspicion.

A reward was advertised in the newspaper. £300 for information on the robbed gold. Not a bad reward, I'd have been tempted to tell on them.

Agar and Pierce planned to melt down the gold bars to make smaller bars so they would be less suspicious, and probably so they'd be easier to carry. The first round of bullion was sold and split between Agar, Pierce, Tester and Burgess.

Agar got himself arrested for cheque fraud in an unrelated crime to the gold robbery. I'm not sure why he felt the need to continue a life of crime after the train robbery. A villain can't change his eyebrows I suppose.

He was sentenced to life imprisonment, so Agar did the noble
thing and asked Pierce to give his money, around £7,000, to Fanny Kay to support her and his child. Pierce agreed but double crossed his mate and kept the money for himself.

Kay fell on hard times and made the discovery that Pierce had stolen her money, so she marched her way over to the governor of Newgate Prison and confessed she knew about the gold robbery and who had done it. She gave the names of William Pierce, James Burgess, and William Tester. On learning that Pierce had double crossed him Agar supported Kay's statement.

Towards the end of 1856, a year and a half after the robbery had actually taken place, Pierce, Burgess, and Tester were arrested. There was a reunion early in 1857 in the courtroom where Agar and Kay testified against the other three. Agar owned up to the whole thing, taking his three former mates with him.

If Pierce had only had the decency to not double cross his friend and help a mother and her child, then this crime would undoubtably have gone unsolved. Let that be a lesson to you all– if you ever rob a load of gold with your friends, don't double cross them.

Not that I'm a walking advertisement for the Railway Museum but you can see one of the bullion boxes there. (At least you can at the time of writing this book) So if this story has perked your interest, maybe go check it out.

London Underground

Do you know what's cooler than building railways above ground? Building railways underground. And that's exactly what came to London in 1863. People were calling it the eighth wonder of the world. But you can bet your bottom dollar that it wasn't as simple as you might think. This chapter is all about the unromantic truth of the London Underground.

The London Underground does have a pretty cool claim to fame as it was the first of its kind in the world. Everyone loves to brag about something. Despite this achievement everyone seems to have chosen to forget about the roughly 15,000 people who had their homes destroyed.

The first underground trains ran between Paddington and Farringdon and used gas-lit wooden carriages, which were still opened by hand as there were no electric doors back then. You won't be surprised to learn that the carriages were pulled by steam locomotives.

Can you imagine how smelly that first journey would have been? You're in a tunnel filled with gas and steam. What a way to travel. Even today it doesn't smell very pleasant when you're on the underground network. Despite the smell, around 40,000 passengers were transported on the opening day.

I jest about the smell, but it was a serious problem that engineers had to solve. To reduce the steam, they fit special pipes to the locomotives to send the steam which would normally come out of the chimney into tanks of cold water which were fitted on the side of the locomotives. They also started to use coke instead of coal- Coke produces less smoke than coal. Despite these efforts, smoke was still a massive problem in the Underground, and it would remain a massive issue until the Underground was electrified in the 1900s.

Pollution was probably at its worst in the Thames tunnel which was bought by the underground in the late 1860s. On the 7th of January 1869 the steam train ran through the famous Thames tunnel but because it was built without ventilation to let the smoke out and it was under the river the smoke of the trains had nowhere to go.

The Underground was built using what is called the "cut and cover" method. To make life easier they decided the underground should follow the original route of the existing roads. The cut and cover method meant they would rip up the road, dig down, build the section of track and tunnel, cover it back up, then rebuild the road of top. Your guess is as good as mine as to why they chose such a disruptive method to the rest of London life. I want to say that money was somehow involved.

London was mostly one big building site in Victorian times, so I suppose having one more road dug up made little difference to the residents. Some projects took years to complete as the money kept running out. It seems odd that the idea of the Underground was to reduce congestion on the street, but it probably caused more congestion while it was being built.

You also have to remember that back in the 1860s when they were building the Underground there were no big tunnel boring machines to help and the tools available were only very basic. The navvies had to shift an unreal amount of dirt, and many lost their lives or received a serious injury.

There were boiler explosions of the steam engines helping to clear the dirt, the tunnels would often flood as they were being dug and you were never safe from potential tunnel collapse.

The navvies caused a lot of trouble in London with their extracurricular activities. Most of their drinking parties ended in brawls. Unfortunately, where there were navvies there were problems. The railway companies needed them to do the heavy work though, so they very rarely tried to control their workforce.

Along with the pollution and actually building the tunnels there was another question to be answered: How were the passengers going to get to the stations underground? Stairs were the first solution but in 1890 they installed hydraulic lifts. They were big, slow, heavy machines which used water to move the lifts up and down.

The first underground electric railway opened in 1890 and ran from King William Street in the City of London, under the River

Thames and ended up in Stockwell. I don't live in London so I'm just saying names at this point. I'd suggest getting a map of London.

It's slightly outside the Victorian timeline but I want to very quickly mention a couple of things which happened in 1908. It was a good year for the Underground. In fact, it was the first time the name Underground first appeared in the stations, and it was the first year that the circle logo which we all recognise as the logo of the London Underground was used. I also want to add that it in 1911 the Underground got its first ever escalator at Earl's Court station.

I know this is the unromantic railways and we want to hear all about all the things that went wrong but believe it or not they actually did a pretty good job on the Underground – as long as you ignore all those made homeless of course.

Daddy Long Legs

The Victorian era saw weird and wonderful inventions, and none were quite as weird as what was bought to life by Brighton born and bred inventor named Magnus Volk in 1896. Don't worry if you don't like bugs because I'm not talking about a real daddy Long-legs.

Volk had already invented the country's first electric railway in 1833- which feels like a strange thing to just brush over but I'm going to- so he knew the only way to live up to the expectations of his new railway line was to make it run through the sea. He put the carriage on large stilts, so it was high above the water. Quickly, it got the nickname "Daddy Long-Legs". The actual name of the carriage was Pioneer.

I'm not really sure how to describe Pioneer without using up four-hundred and three pages so here's a picture instead.

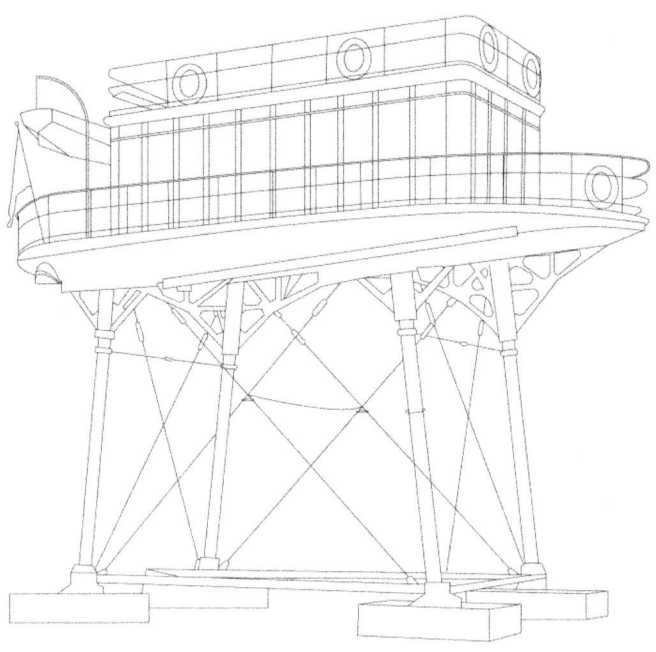

The mental image of a train carriage on stilts is actually hilarious. What do you think is funnier- a carriage on stilts or a carriage on a unicycle?

Pioneer first ran on the 28th of November 1896- you can imagine the craned necks as it ran through the sea. I can guarantee at least one person thought it was a terrible remake of Godzilla- actually why didn't Volk call it something cool like Godzilla?

What's really cool is that Volk didn't let water get in the way of his electric dream, so Pioneer was still powered by electricity. It had what was effectively a pantograph (the thing you see on top of trains today) which drew electricity from the wire which ran parallel with the tracks. Let that be a lesson to you all- never let the potential electrocution of your passengers stand in your way.

Actually, brief science lesson (sorry!) Pure water doesn't actually conduct electricity. It's the salt and other stuff which is dissolved in it that conducts the electricity. Pioneer was in the sea which has salt in it so if something had gone really wrong passengers could have been electrocuted so therefore my attempted humour still stands. Ha!

Speaking of the sea, because Pioneer ran through the sea it had to be driven a qualified boat captain. It was also fitted with a lifeboat and had a few lifebelts to go with it. I wonder if they were ever tempted to install a diving board.

One thing Pioneer wasn't going to break was any speed records. It travelled at a dawdling pace to put it kindly. The motors were underpowered, and they couldn't afford newer ones. This meant it could only run-in shallow water- the tide would be too strong, and it wouldn't move if they went too deep. Any plans on building an open-air carriage to France were dashed yet again.

In fairness, the railway was fairly successful. About 45,000 passengers enjoyed a journey in the second half of 1897. That's a lot of people. Then world needs more ideas like this- people play it too safe too often. I'm willing to be a shareholder if anyone wants to rebuild the Pioneer- hook me up.

Things sadly did go wrong for Pioneer (it didn't electrocute anyone, don't worry). A massive storm a week or so after launch broke the new invention but thanks to some expert salvaging skills the Pioneer was repaired and was back in action in July 1897. The track got damaged which meant it couldn't run for some of 1900 and it had its time was cut short when Brighton Council wanted to build new sea defences, so it was out of business in 1901.

I'm not sure if I've said anything about this already because this is one of the last bits of the book I'm writing, but I'm placing on record right now that if a time machine gets invented and I can only go back and travel on one thing in Victorian Britain- I choose the daddy-long-legs. What would you choose?

Trains of the dead

London had a big problem. All the graveyards were filling up and the railways were taking over the city. Coffins were literally being stacked on top of each other. There were even graveyards where the coffins weren't buried properly so you could see parts of them sticking out the dirt. Some reports suggest up to 20 people could be buried in the same grave.

Building the London Underground didn't help the situation. As they tunnelled under the city, they disturbed the graveyards and sent the remains of people's loved ones spilling all over the road. There was a problem before you even throw the citywide sewer redevelopment into the mix.

At any rate, London was getting full and the graves were overflowing. Something needed to be done, and quickly. The idea was to open up graves and cemeteries outside of the city. Brookwood Cemetery in Surrey came into being. To this day it remains one of the largest cemeteries in Europe. You will already have guessed but the way they were going to get the bodies there was by rail.

The new London Necropolis Company ran trains out of Waterloo station to Brookwood Cemetery. The first train departed on the 13th of November 1854. I checked and that was a Monday, not a Friday. A train full of dead bodies leaving on Friday 13th sounds like a horror film waiting to happen – I'm going to copyright that idea now just in case I want to come back to it.

Waterloo was a great location for such a station, mostly because it was close to the river so bodies could be quickly and cheaply transported to the station using the water. Again, I'm using some guesswork, but I think they used a boat to transport the bodies on the river. They didn't just let them float to Waterloo on their own. It also had good road connections.

Leaving from Waterloo meant you had a better view on the train out of the city. Did I mention that mourners would travel with the coffin? I don't think I did- for a moment I bet you thought they were considering the dead people's window view.

Victorians sometimes had bells put next to their grave which they could ring from underground should they have been mistakenly buried alive. Another horror story idea just hit me- one of the graveyard bells rings but when they dig up the grave it's empty. Copyright- my idea.

Perhaps the railway company wanted to give the coffins a good view in case one of them came back and complained about it. They'd do anything for a 5-star review. (Speaking of 5-star reviews- have you reviewed this book yet?)

For some unknown reason you could pay to get your loved ones coffin its own compartment on the train. That's right folks, there was a first, second, and third-class ticket for coffins. A first-class ticket gave you a choice of the best plots in the cemetery and would cost you roughly £2 10 shillings- just £240 in today's money. Second class would cost £1 (£96 today) and third-class were cheap as chips at only 2 shillings (£10 today). The slight downfall to a third-class ticket would that the grave wouldn't be given a stone to mark them.

The Victorians were so dedicated to the class system they didn't even want their dead mixing with the lower classes. There was no survey done at the time, but I bet the dead wouldn't have had any issues who they shared a compartment with.

The new Necropolis railway actually made pretty good business. It was heavily involved in the relocation of the London burial grounds. With all the engineering projects taking place nearly 10,000 bodies were displaced. They were packed into 220 huge containers and moved to the new graveyard in Brookwood.

For some context each of these large containers would have contained around 26 adults plus children- not the sort of package someone would want to open without knowing what was in it. By the time the company was closed down they'd helped relocate around 25 London burial grounds to make way for developments.

Despite the promising start the company met a dead end (pun intended) when it came to moving enough bodies every year. They had originally planned to be moving between 20 and 50 thousand bodies by rail each year. This never happened as they only averaged about 2,500 bodies per year. Not good when it came to keeping the company afloat and profitable.

The end of the railway came in 1941 when it was massively

damaged by an air raid during the Second World War. The company never reopened and only the old office buildings of the London Necropolis railway still exist today but is used as a different company's offices.

The Brookwood Cemetery is still in use today and has some fairly notable people buried there. Top of the list is probably a former king of England called Edward the Martyr- his grave was taken from Shaftesbury Abbey to Brookwood in 1984.

So not only did the railways transport people who were alive they also transported the dead. Which train would you have preferred to have travelled on? That's a silly question- everyone would prefer to travel on the train which carried people who were alive- forget I asked such a stupid question.

Many royal coffins have been transported by the railways- including Queen Victorias. The train still plays an important part in the state funeral today.

The Armagh rail disaster

Unfortunately, the reason the railways were unromantic is mostly because of the huge number of accidents that took place. Way too many people lost their lives because of poor engineering, rejection of health and safety, and just plain stupidity. The Armagh rail disaster can be put down to lots of different errors. Here's the story of what happened in Northern Ireland that day.

On the morning of the 12th of June 1889 members of an Armagh Methodist Sunday School were boarding a train which was taking them for a day trip to the seaside resort of Warrenpoint. A special train had been organised and, on the morning, more passengers turned up than the 800 originally planned.

Wanting to avoid complaints the station master decided to put an extra two carriages onto the train. This meant there was 15 carriages to fit a total of about 940 passengers into. There are some suggestions that the driver of the train asked for an extra locomotive to help pull the train to the seaside resort, but the station master apparently refused.

Not adding a second locomotive was the first mistake- well second if you count the fact it was silly to add an extra two carriages. The track leading to the resort was at a upward gradient, so two locomotives would have solved a major problem they come across later on.

I won't go into the science of why inclines and steam locomotives don't get along with each other as it involves talking about how the wheels don't have tyres on so there's very little friction in between the track and the wheels so the locomotives can't grip when they're trying to go uphill- Oh I just explained it, oops.

Back to the story. As the train started chugging up the incline- it was going slowly but it was still moving. At least it was moving until it got within 100 metres of the top of the incline, where it stalled. It didn't have enough puff to get up the rest of the hill. The driver put the brakes on to stop the train rolling back down the hill.

Let's pause the story again so I quickly explain brakes to you- I should have said let's put the brakes on the story.

At the end of the 1800s a new invention was created which allowed the driver to turn the brakes on every carriage from the cab. Trains use them today and they're what we call vacuum brakes.

I won't go through the science of what a vacuum is because nobody wants to read about how a vacuum is something where there is no air like in space.

Vacuum brakes work by sucking all the air out of the system which lets the brakes turn off and away you go. When you let air back into the system the brakes are put back on. Clever right? It means that if you have a leaky pipe the train brakes turn on and the train stops. Then everyone gets slightly embarrassed because the train can't move until you fix the hole in the pipe.

Unfortunately, and as you may already have guessed, the train with 940 passengers- most of which were children- on didn't have this type of vacuum brakes. It had the opposite. On this train when you let air into the system it turns off the brakes and when you suck the air out it puts the brakes on. I'm sure you've realised why this is easily mistake number 2 and perhaps the dumbest brake system ever. If you get a leak in your pipe the brakes are stuck off so you can't put the brakes on the carriages.

So, we now have a train that has stalled carrying 940 passengers almost at the top of a hill. It obviously couldn't stay there so the train crew had two choices.

Choice 1- Send a runner back to the station to get the next train to slowly pull up behind the train and push them up the rest of the hill.

Choice 2- Unhook the first five carriages and pull them up the hill to the nearest station, then come back for the final ten carriages which would be held on the hill by the guard's van brake at the back.

Whichever choice was chosen the passengers couldn't have gotten out the train to watch as the doors had been locked once they'd had their tickets checked. But the passengers all pushing would probably have been a reasonable suggestion.

I'm genuinely curious which option you would have chosen if you had been there that day. My first recommendation would have been getting the passengers out of the train before doing anything.

The crew chose choice 2 (try and say that 10 times quickly). They used rocks and stones as a wedge behind the guard's van and made sure the vans brakes were firmly applied. These brakes in the guard's van weren't controlled by the driver.

The disconnected the first 5 carriages which let air into the brake system and turned all the carriage brakes off. This meant that 10 carriages were being kept on the hill by the brake in the guard's van and a few piles of rocks.

With it's now lighter load the driver returned to the locomotive and began the task of pulling the first five carriages up the rest of the hill. As they set off the train rolled backwards slightly before moving forward. This slight movement backwards was enough to unwedge the rocks behind the guard's van wheels and shatter its brake. The back 10 carriages of the train rolled down the hill as the first five carriages went upwards. Realising this the driver desperately tried to reverse the front of half of the train but they couldn't catch the runaway rear section.

The train which had departed after the now runaway train was cruising at 25mph when the driver saw the oncoming runaway carriages. The driver braked to reduce the speed to around 5mph but there was no chance of stopping the runaway train with a broken guard's brake and it had now potentially reached 30mph. There was nothing to stop the collision which occurred.

Most of the runaway carriages ended up taking a fall down the 14-metre high embarkment. 80 people lost their lives and another 260 were injured.

The most frustrating thing is that this never should have happened and could have prevented. You might wonder how?

- Using a bigger locomotive that was strong enough to pull the 15 carriages.
- Not locking the passengers in the carriages and letting them get out.

- Putting both brake vans at the back of the train- one had been behind the locomotive. If they'd both been at the back it would have meant the carriages would have had two brakes to hold them once they'd been separated.
- Not having 15 carriages on the train which was only ever meant to be 13 carriages long.
- Not having a braking system which turned the brakes off when air was in the system.

You see how frustrating it is? How easy it would have been to have stopped something like this ever happening?

The slimmest of silver lining is that the government finally passed a law that required companies to install the proper vacuum brakes- the one where brakes turn on with air in the system- on their trains. But why did it take an accident like this before they enforced it?

To say the Armagh rail disaster was avoidable is a massive understatement, it was the worst railway disaster that happened during the 19th century and even to this day is considered the worst ever railway disaster to have happened in Ireland. Railway carelessness was costing lives, and finally the government stepped in and enforced health and safety rules, stopping companies cutting corners- legally anyway.

Brilliant Brunel's

It would be borderline illegal for me to go through this book without talking at least a little bit about Isambard Kingdom Brunel. I have little doubt you'll know his name. I'm going to sandwich the Brunel chapter in between 2 stories of accidents to try to lighten the mood slightly.

Isambard was responsible for the building of many famous ships (S.S Great Britain, Great Western and Great Eastern to name a few). He also built bridges (Clifton Suspension Bridge, Royal Albert bridge and Maidenhead Railway Bridge). He even built tunnels (Box Tunnel). But a little-known fact that Brunel never gets enough credit for. He was possibly the greatest sandcastle builder to ever live.

As well as Isambard, a lot of people forget his father, Marc, was also a top tier engineer who often gets left in his son's shadow. It would have been difficult to be literally in Isambard's shadow- not only because it was Britain and very rarely sunny, but also Isambard was really short so wouldn't have a big shadow. But the engineering shadow Isambard created was huge.

His dad, Marc Isambard Brunel, was taking over an attempt to build a tunnel under the River Thames in London. An inventor and engineer called Richard Trevithick (yep, the guy who built the first steam locomotive) had previously attempted it but had given up.

When I say Trevithick gave up, he didn't just wake up one day and decide he couldn't be bothered; the river waters kept breaking through the attempts of constructing the tunnel. Trevithick's tunnel was almost 30ft long when they abandoned it in an incomplete condition.

Marc Brunel created a tunnelling shield which was used to dig out some of the London Underground. A developed version of his machine, called a boring machine, would dig out the Channel Tunnel, between Folkestone and Calais, which was finished on the 6th of May 1994. (Just 6 days before my third birthday. To this day I still reject the rumours that the tunnel was built as a birthday present to me.)

The tunnelling shield was a giant leap for engineering projects- particularly building tunnels under water. The biggest problem engineers had was that as they were digging out the tunnels under water the sides kept falling in, drowning, and crushing the majority of their workforce.

Britain has a long history of tunnel building accidents. To build tunnels, the navvies and engineers started to use gunpowder- and eventually dynamite when it was invented in the 1870s- to blast through the tougher rocks they were attempting to dig through. Now, you may wonder how the workers got away from the explosions.

As tunnels were built the crew would build ventilation shafts on the top so people could breathe when digging. So they'd load the gunpowder in front of the rock you weren't able to dig through, light the fuse, run back to the bucket which had been lowered down into the tunnel through the ventilation shaft on a long piece of rope, get into the bucket, and trust your colleagues to pull you up and out of the tunnel before it explodes.

There are plenty of reports which suggest this didn't always go as planned- the bucket could get stuck, or the rope could snap, or even just not be pulled up quickly enough to avoid the explosion. It wasn't that uncommon for workers to actually fall out of the bucket.

With this limited information I'm sure you'll agree with me that the tunnel business was incredibly dangerous- but tunnels were really important to the railways, so they kept being built.

For his tunnelling shield, Marc Brunel was apparently inspired by a shipworm which are gross looking worms which eat through the wood on ships. I dare you to google what they look like. The shipworm has a sort of round thing near their head – looks a bit like a shield, which helps them when they're eating their way through the wood. Marc saw this and his engineering brain saw how it could be useful for building tunnels.

Brunel entered intense negotiations with the shipworms to join his workforce but after several stalemates, and worrying suggestions of getting the unions involved, he decided to build a larger metal version. The machine acted like a shield, protecting workers from any collapses in the tunnel whilst the navvies dug out between the gaps at the front. It also meant they could build a tunnel support as they went along.

It was actually very rare seeing someone create something that actually protected the workforce. More often than not the leading engineers didn't care how many people died to see their vision become reality.

Brunel junior joined his father's business in 1822 after two years of studying engineering and maths in France and was present when work began on building the Thames Tunnel in 1825. It wasn't all smooth building and Isambard himself almost drowned when there was a tunnel collapse in 1828. This meant work on the tunnel was stopped.

Eventually the tunnel under the Thames was finished and

opened on the 25th of March 1843. It was only used by foot traffic and almost 25 million people passed through the tunnel (not at the same time).

The first trains travelled through the tunnel in 1869 after it was bought for roughly £200,000, and it's still there today so they clearly built it pretty well. It's actually now part of the London underground.

Marc Brunel passed away on the 7th of October 1849 at the age of 80. His son wouldn't last much longer.

Isambard Brunel- it actually feels weird not using his full name- wasn't satisfied with just building tunnels; he is perhaps best known for building ships. S.S Great Britain was the longest passenger ship in the world between 1845 and 1854 and took passengers between Bristol and New York city. This isn't a book about the not so romantic oceans though so let's move on quickly.

When he wasn't building tunnels or big boats, IKB was designing railway stations. He designed Bristol Temple Meads station which opened in 1841, then was the co-designer of Paddington Station which opened in1854. I've been to both of these stations and can vouch that they're pretty nice stations. The prices at the coffee stands were a rip off but I'm not sure how much Brunel had to do with setting the prices.

He built a few famous bridges which I can't remember the names of, but I know the Royal Albert Bridge was one of them. Brunel also built railways.

He was chief engineer of the Great Western Railway from 1833 and had big plans. And most of these planned on being different to George Stephenson. He helped construct a track between London and Bristol.

One difference was that Brunel built his railways on broad gauge. The gauge is the width of the track. George Stephenson, who had realised before most others that a country connected by the railways would be beneficial, had built his railways on what is now known as standard gauge. This meant most tracks in the country were 4 foot 8 ½ inches wide. Brunel decided broad gauge was better so the railways he helped build were 7ft wide.

Stephenson used the narrower gauge as it was one that had been used when horses and his work in the collieries. Before the invention of the steam locomotives horses had been used transport goods from the mines. To make life easier they dug grooves for the carriage wheels to run through. Some smaller trucks even used to be pushed and pulled on wooden trackways.

Brunel wanted the wider gauge as another way to leave the horse and cart era behind but also because a wider gauge provided far more pleasant, smoother, and faster railway journeys. Image having smoother and faster railway journeys

Because the majority of the railways in Britain got built on the 4ft 8 ½ inch gauge, Brunel's dream of having a country filled with broad gauge was destroyed and broad gauge stopped being built in 1860- a year after Brunel had passed away and all the broad-gauge track had been ripped up and replaced with the smaller standard gauge by 1892. I wonder what the railways would be like today if Brunel had won the battle of the gauges...

IKB died at the age of just 53 on the 15th of September 1859- just a month before his good friend Robert Stephenson also passed away. 1859 was a sad year for losing notable Victorian engineers.

Charles Dickens and the Staplehurst rail crash

The railways had their fair share of accidents. In fact, I could write a whole book dedicated to the crashes, disasters, and accidents on the railways. (Possible future book?)

One accident I want to tell you about is one that involves someone you've almost definitely heard of (or at least read in the chapter title) Charles Dickens.

Charles Dickens was born on the 7th of February 1812 in Portsmouth to a mum called Elizabeth and a dad called John. He's most famous for writing some of the world's most famous books. A Christmas Carol, Oliver Twist, David Copperfield, Great Expectations and Bleak House to name but a few. You'll probably hear about how wonderful all his books are when you're at school.

Charles loved the railways at first. They allowed him to travel quickly around the country to all the book readings he was asked to do. He even wrote a book called "The Signal-Man" which followed a railway signalman who was being haunted by a ghost.

Anyway, enough of writing a history lesson to get the word count up, let's get onto the part everyone's interested in, the railway crash.

I'm sure you're well aware that an important part of the railways is the track itself. Without the rail we would just be calling the railways "ways".

On the particular day that the boat train (not a boat on tracks, a boat train was a passenger train which took people to ports to catch a ship. To clarify they didn't catch the ship with a fishing rod, they got out of the boat train and walked onto the ship) was travelling back to London from Folkestone the engineers had pulled up roughly twelve metres of tracks on a three-metre-tall wooden bridge which crossed the River Beult. The technical name for this is "engineering works".

We're all intelligent people and know that taking up a piece of track when a train is coming down the track is not a good idea in the slightest. Trains don't move anywhere without tracks so not having tracks creates a problem.

When completing engineering works the engineers were required to place a red flag 900 metres down the track. This meant the driver had plenty of warning there were engineering works ahead and they could safely stop the train. On this day however the person sent out to place the red flag was obviously feeling a little bit lazy and could only be bothered to walk out about 500 metres. This means that when the driver saw the red flag to warn about the engineering works there wasn't enough time to stop the train. It was travelling about thirty miles per hour when it reached the removed section of track.

Now you're probably wondering why the engineer would remove a section of track when there was a train due to travel across it. It was a calamitous example of human error. The foreman (the person in charge of the workers) misread the railway timetable and the train which carried Charles Dickens arrived far earlier than he thought it would.

The train was carrying 85 first-class and 35 second-class passengers and when it reached the missing piece of track the locomotive, it's tender and one of the carriages made it across. The back two carriages didn't travel across and remained on the track. Sadly, the middle carriages fell the three metres into the riverbed after the wooden slats of the bridge collapsed under the weight of the train.

Of the 120 passengers on board 10 lost their lives and a further 40 people were injured (some sources suggest it was closer to 60 people who were injured). Charles Dickens was in a first-class carriage which hadn't fallen onto the riverbed, but it was sticking over the edge. He climbed out of the window of his carriage and did his part to help the injured and some of those who lost their lives died in his arms.

This whole experience made Dickens exceptionally nervous about travelling by rail and he did everything in his power to avoid travelling on them again, even if it meant the journey taking longer and being less comfortable. Apparently, he actually lost his voice for the 2 weeks following the crash.

Charles Dickens passed away in 1870, aged 58, five years to the day after the Staplehurst rail crash. Many suggest he never fully recovered from the crash, and it haunted him for the final 5 years of his life.

No more chapter titles

I'm going to be honest. I'm completely out of chapter titles. You might think- YES that means the book is over!

If this is what you were thinking, I'm afraid you're wrong. Dead wrong. So wrong that you can't even see the right answer. And to be honest if you're still reading at this point you are clearly enjoying the book.

This chapter is going to be like a speed round. I'm just going to throw facts at you and it's your job to dramatically catch them. If you want to make it a proper speed round you could read the next few pages as quickly as possible. An even bigger challenge would be to try and read it in one breath.

Ready?

1) In 1783 Manchester had 1 cotton mill and a population of 24,000 people. Because of the railways by the time the mid 1830's rolled around it had 86 cotton mills and a population of 150,000 people! This made Manchester the world's first industrial city.

2) George Stephenson couldn't read or write. He tried to learn several times but was never fluent in either discipline. This meant he was very reliant on his son, Robert.

3) You don't really hear the "clickety-clack" sound of the railways anymore. Before the invention of stronger machines that place the track down, all track was laid using the navvies and manual labour. They could only lift shorted bits of track at a time, so the network was built up of lots of smaller bits of tracks which were joined together. There were small gaps between each section and as the wheels went over them you got the "clickety-clack" sound. The track sections are much longer now so the "clickety-clack" sound has almost disappeared from existence.

4) In order to get permission to build a railway, you had to send a petition to parliament in London. They would review the costs and make sure it was viable to make. Many railway investors kept a pot of money to one side to bribe MPs to make sure their railway could be built. This made the job of carrying the petition and new railway plans an incredibly dangerous occupation.

5) Rival companies would get word that someone was trying to build a railway which would impact their own and would go as far as killing people carrying railway plans to stop them being built. One company in Sheffield was desperate for their proposed railway to be built. To ensure the rival companies couldn't intercept the plans they put on a fake funeral and hid the plans inside the coffin. The coffin was

then transported to London by train and received at the other end. It's incredible the lengths to which companies had to go to ensure their railway would be built. Sorry, I don't know if the railway was built or not.

6) A man called William Henry Smith created a company called WH Smith in 1792. When the London to Birmingham railway opened, they opened a store on Euston Station in 1848. It didn't take long until they had stores on stations all over the country, within 15 years there were 500 hundred stores across the railways. Even nowadays it's very rare to go to a railway station and not see a WH Smiths.

Rather than selling books at expensive prices the WH Smith stores sold books that even the poor people could afford. Some of the previously published books might cost 6 weeks wages of an average worker. All of a sudden poor people could learn from books- you can imagine the rich people reacted negatively to this. WH Smith actually helped bring a social revolution to the country.

7) When the railways were first built their job of keeping to a timetable was made even more difficult by the fact that every town would be on a separate different time. Greenwich Mean Time was adopted by the railways, so all their timetables synced up.

8) Between 1840 and 1850 there were around 50,000 bridges built in Britain as part of the new railways. These bridges needed around 300,000 bricks each. It would have been a good time to be a brick maker.

9) Timothy Hackworth built a locomotive for the Russian government in 1836. Not bad for someone who lived in Stephenson's shadow.

10) You used to have to buy a train ticket for your dog. It would cost you half fare which is the same as a children's ticket. Dogs used to sit in the guard's van at the back of the train. I hope the guard was dog person.

11) There were no signals on the first railway tracks. They used policemen on the stations to make sure trains didn't get too close together. Each officer would have a timetable and would only allow a train to leave the station if the one before had been gone for at least 10 minutes.

12) There were 6 different railway companies in the city of Manchester alone. They shared stations but had different platforms. They were competing for all the same passengers This led to a massive rivalry between the companies. This rivalry led to literal fights between the companies, posters being torn down, property defaced and even passengers being arrested for being on a platform with a ticket for the wrong company. Perhaps most annoying though was that there wasn't a direct train to take you from the North to the South of the city. Passengers had to keep changing trains to get across the city.

13) Thomas Cook took 500 teetotallers from Leicester to Loughborough. He negotiated cheaper prices with the railway company. This kickstarted a whole host of special excursion trains. The prices of these trains were much cheaper, and the public snapped them up. There were journeys to the seaside, to the football, and even to public hangings.

14) There was a railway accident on the 3rd of May 1833 where a train collided with a farmer's cart on the level crossing. This led to the locomotive whistle being placed on locomotives so they could toot them to warn people of their impending arrival.

15) The railways are full of a wide range of colours, with a lot of awesome names. Garter Blue, Brunswick Green and some more that I honestly can't remember. Black and red! But the greatest colour on the railways was called "Improved Engine Green" – it was going to be the greatest colour ever created. The slight problem was the person who designed it was colour blind so what he thought was Improved Engine Green was actually a fairly disturbing colour brown- like I've eaten a lot of curry poo brown... Why didn't anyone tell him it wasn't green? He was the boss of the paint factory, and everyone was too afraid to argue as they were afraid that they'd lose their jobs.

16) The first recorded accident involving someone being drunk on the railways was on the 26th of March 1831. The drunken gentleman attempted to jump on a full speed train- like 20 mph- as it went through a station. Needless to say, he didn't jump into the carriage like a hero but ended up on the track with extremely sore legs after the carriages ran over them. His legs were amputated but I think he survived.

17) Timothy Hackworth built a locomotive called Sans Pereil 2 – in fact this was the last locomotive he ever designed- and challenged Robert Stephenson to a race between York and Berwick (on the Scotland border). Stephenson declined.

18) Dogs were commonly used on stations in the Victorian era. Money collecting boxes were strapped to their backs and

they'd wander the platforms collecting money for varies charities.

19) Between 1845 and 1901 over £3 billion was spent building the railways. That sounds like a lot of money nowadays let alone back then. That's about £384,534,433,797 in today's money – I'll be completely honest I have no idea what that number even is. Let's go with it's a lot of money- that sounds good... it is a lot of money.

20) I think I've said it 1000 times, but everything was transported by the railways- even coffins. The Station Masters at stations decided it wouldn't be a good look to have coffins laying around the stations. The coffin carrier- basically a box on wheels- was invented to hold up to three coffins inside. Everyone knew what was in them- but it was better than having to look at a load of coffins. These coffins would ride in guards van with the guard. There is a story where the train went over a particularly bumpy piece of track and several coffins spilled out onto the track and went everywhere- grim...

21) A "popular" game in Victorian Britain was to wear your finest white shirt and stand on a bridge. You would wait for a steam train to pass underneath and whoever got the dirtiest shirt from the soot and smoke of the train would win.

22) Another one for my nephew, Phoenix. The locomotive named after him – despite it being build 150 years before he was born- was involved in an accident in 1831. A plank of wood had been stupidly left across the track by a group of work people. When Phoenix hit it, it caused a locomotive to assistant to be hurled from the loco and onto the track where he got his head squished by the carriages. I have no evidence, but I think he died quickly.

23) The oldest surviving steam locomotive built sometime between 1813 and 1814 is called Puffing Billy. If anyone is desperately interested the second oldest surviving steam locomotive is called the Wylam Dilly built in 1815 by William Headley and Timothy Hackworth. If that doesn't satisfy your thirst for knowledge the third oldest surviving steam locomotive is called Billy. It was built in 1816 by George Stephenson. The fourth steam locomotive is for you to find out for yourself because I have no idea.

24) The world's oldest steam locomotive to still run is called "Fairy Queen". It was built at Leeds in 1855 and is still in full working order in India today. (True at the time of writing at least- if it's stopped running when you're reading this then cross this fact out with a pen).

25) The world's first recorded railway station was in Swansea, it started passenger services in 1807- but rather than steam locomotives pulling the carriages they used horses. The oldest existing station is the Liverpool Road station which opened on the 15th September 1830 then the oldest railway station still to be in operation is Broad Green station in Liverpool which opened on the same day. In case you were wondering why they aren't known as the joint oldest it's because the buildings at Broad Green date from 1970 whilst the ones at Liverpool Road are still the original buildings.

People you should probably know

The railway world was filled with hundreds and thousands of people who should be given credit for playing a part in its success. But, as much as I want to write a five hundred-thousand-page book, we don't have room for them all- and I don't have the energy to check how to spell all of their names.

Over the next few pages, I've added some more information and short biographies of some of the big players in the Victorian railway world. It would be another six thousand pages if I was to mention everyone who deserves to be mentioned, so I apologise to everyone I've not spoken about- maybe in future books.

Queen Victoria

Queen Alexandrina Victoria was born on the 24th of May 1819 at Kensington Palace, London. (Kensington Palace is where Prince William and Kate live nowadays- or at least in 2022 they did!)

She became Queen in 1837 when her uncle, William IV, died in the early hours of the morning on the 20th of June. She was coronated a year later on the 28th of June 1838 at Westminster Abbey. Over 400,000 people arrived in London for celebrations. (I think 4 people came to my last birthday party- Victoria appears to have been more popular than me.)

Because Victoria was unmarried, she had to live with her mum as all unmarried ladies had to back then. Imagine being Queen and still having to live with your mum! Victoria found her mum a room in Buckingham Palace and refused to see her.

She married Albert in 1840. She proposed to him, rather than the other way round, because no one is allowed to propose to the reigning monarch. They married at St. James' Palace cathedral and would go onto have 9 children- Victoria, Edward, Alice, Alfred, Helena, Louise, Arthur, Leopold, and Beatrice.

Victoria and Albert were very popular and made plenty of public appearances. They opened factories, railways, and hospitals throughout their reign together.

She became the first reigning monarch to ride on the railways in 1842 and enjoyed travelling on them for convenience (and to make the drivers life difficult and considerably more stressful).

Victoria and Albert shared a mutual love of the arts and in 1851 the Great Exhibition took place. Prince Albert and Henry Cole organised the whole thing. It was the first international "world fair" style event. People like Charles Dickens, Charles Darwin, and Charlotte Bronte visited. The V & A museum opened as a result of the Great Exhibition and the royal couple were big supporters.

Sadly, Prince Albert passed away in 1861 and Victoria was, understandably, heartbroken. She wore a black dress and a widow's cap for the remainder of her reign. She never neglected her royal duties but rarely appeared in public until the 1870's.

Victoria was the survivor of 8 assassination attempts, the first of which came only four months after being married. A man called Edward Oxford. The 18-year-old took a shot at Victoria and Albert as they left Buckingham Palace in a carriage. Despite being close to the carriage, Oxford luckily missed his first shot. He had barely a chance to fire the second before the crowd tackled him to the ground. Oxford was arrested and spent the next 24 years in an insane asylum before being deported to Australia.

Assassination attempts on Queen Victoria

1- Edward Oxford- 1st of June 1840
2- John Francis- 29th of May 1842
3- John Francis- 30th of May 1842
4- John William Bean- 3rd July 1842
5- William Hamilton- 19th of June 1849
6- Robert Pate- 27th June 1850
7- Arthur O'Connor- 29th February 1872
8- Roderick Maclean- 2nd March 1882

There were more than likely more assassination attempts, but these are the only ones we know about.

She was ruler when some of the biggest inventions were created. Inventions like the telephone, photography, the pedal bicycle, petrol, the sewing machine, safety matches, Jelly Babies, electricity, the comic book, chocolate easter eggs, the typewriter, electric light bulb- there are more but my hands hurt from typing.

Queen Victoria passed away at the age of 81, on the 22nd of January 1901 on the Isle of Wight. Her 63-year and seven-month reign makes her the second longest serving monarch behind Queen Elizabeth II. She is buried with her husband in the Frogmore Mausoleum.

Honestly, there have been hundreds of books and articles written on Queen Victoria so if you fancy learning more about good old Queen Victoria you have plenty of sources to choose from.

Robert Stephenson

Robert Stephenson was born on the 16th of October 1803 and had a fairly famous father. Robert was great friends with one Isambard Kingdom Brunel. They had their differences- mostly over what width the track should be, but the two great engineers were friends until the very end. They passed away within one month of each other.

Robert had a good education in Newcastle and then the University of Edinburgh before receiving his first experience of the railways in 1821 when he helped his father survey the Stockton and Darlington Railway.

He went to Colombia in 1824 - I'd imagine working closely with your father would be irksome - to be a mining engineer. A doctor had also suggested that a move to the warmer climate would be good for his health- he'd been relieved from a mining apprenticeship when he was 18 because of trouble with his lungs.

The miners Stephenson was in charge of were difficult folks to manage from Cornwall. They refused to listen to the young engineer and did everything they could to undermine him. They partied hard so not everyone could work, Stephenson reported this to the office in London, but his complaints fell on deaf ears. Robert got ill and travelled to Cartegena, a Columbian port when his contract expired in 1827.

While waiting for his ship to New York, Stephenson met Richard Trevithick and lent him £50 for the journey home. The ship Stephenson boarded to New York got stuck in a storm and sank. Everyone on the ship survived but Robert's luggage and money were lost to the sea. Turns out very few British engineers got any luck in South America.

Whilst getting to the lifeboats Stephenson saw that some second-class passengers got on them before first-class passengers. After some investigation Robert learnt these passengers were freemasons. On learning this he became a freemason when he arrived in New York.

Stephenson's trip to New York was more of a holiday as he

spent his time being a tourist and travelling to see Niagara Falls. He then caught a ship from New York to Liverpool and landed back in Britain in November 1827.

The three years he spent in Colombia were amongst the worst in his father's railway career, proving to the public that Robert was the true mastermind- though history prefers to remember it differently. He helped design and build Rocket on his return to Britain and eventually won the Rainhill trials in 1829. I won't retell the story of the Rainhill trials- it was the first chapter after all.

After Rocket there was no stopping Robert, who appeared to want to distance himself from his father. He won a contract to build a 120-mile railway from London to Birmingham. He was even paid £1500 a year. It wasn't without trouble but the London to Brimingham Railway opened in 1837.

In 1835, Robert and his father George were invited to Belgium where they advised King Leopold on the Belgian railway. Robert was given the "Order of Leopold" which was effectively a knighthood. He would return to Belgium in 1837 when they opened the railway line between Brussels and Ghent. Robert didn't work on the Belgium railway project because his contract with the London to Birmingham railway forbade it- but he was still an active consultant.

Like his good friend Brunel, Robert was also involved in bridge building. His first bridge was an iron bridge which opened in 1846. It travelled over the River Dee near Chester and in 1847 it collapsed when a passenger train was going over it. The locomotive with the driver and fireman on was fine. But everything from the tender backwards fell into the river. Not a great start to his bridge building career.

The other bridges Robert was involved with, the Britannia Bridge and the high-level bridge in Newcastle, were much more successful.

Robert somehow even ended up in the world of politics. He was elected as an MP for Whitby in 1847 and was never voted out. He was a member of the Conservative Paty- probably because of his friendship with the railway king George Hudson.

If almost drowning near New York wasn't enough Robert was involved in a railway crash. A few days after attending his father's funeral in 1848 Robert Stephenson was travelling back home. At Conwy station a carriage had been left overhanging the mainline. The train carrying Stephenson collided with the overhanging carriage. Luckily Stephenson survived.

Robert passed away on the 12th of October 1859. He's buried in Westminster Abbey alongside a whole host of big names, such as Charles Dickens, Charles Darwin, and Isaac Newton. There are more people buried in Westminster Abbey, but it seems a bit morbid to make a list- look it up if you're interested and sorry if I didn't mention your relative who's might be buried there.

Isambard Kingdom Brunel

Isambard Kingdom Brunel is a name famous in engineering circles. He's probably famous in epic hat circles as well. Even if you don't know why he's famous you'll probably have heard his name before.

Brunel was born on the 9th of April 1806 in Portsmouth. He had French heritage as his father had fled to America during the French revolution (1779-1789) before moving to Britain in 1799.

Brunel's mother, Sophia, was actually arrested as an English spy in France and was almost executed. She wasn't executed though and moved to Britain in 1795.

Burnel had two sisters, Sophia, and Emma, who were both older than him. But it was Brunel himself who became the famous one of the siblings.

His father, Marc, was also a pretty notable engineer, but his top hat game always fell short in comparison to his son. He was knighted by Queen Victoria in 1841 though so that's a fair thing to brag about.

Isambard travelled to France in 1820 to study engineering and maths before joining his dad's business in 1822- apparently 2 years of study in France was enough for this whizz kid.

He almost drowned while helping to build the Thames Tunnel in 1828- there was a tunnel collapse, luckily, he had his giant hat to hold onto. Imagine how different the Victorian world would have been if he had drowned that day.

It's difficult to overstate how busy Isambard was during his life. He threw himself into countless projects and I'm not sure when he ever got chance to sit back and relax. Here is a collection of stuff he got up to.

He won a bridge building competition in 1831- his design would become the Clifton suspension bridge. The bridge didn't open until 1864- 5 years after he'd passed away, meaning he never saw it opened. It was built by his colleagues who decided the bridge should be built to honour their fallen friend's memory.

He was appointed chief engineer of the Great Western Railway in 1833 and started to push forward his plans for a broad-gauge railway. His famous Box Tunnel on the London to Bristol railway was the longest in the world when it first opened, just under 2-miles long.

He never shied away from challenges- he helped design and construct the S.S Great Britain and in 1838 it travelled from Liverpool to New York in 13 days.

Along with building railways and tunnels Brunel also got into station design. Work on his own designed Bristol Temple Meads Station in 1841- alongside the Box Tunnel opening. Brunel also co-designed Paddington Station which opened in 1854.

He had been a heavy smoker throughout his life and suffered a stroke on the 5th of September. He passed away ten days later on the 15th of September 1859.

Writing small biographies about people of the past is always a sad event- it always ends with them dying.

George Hudson

George Hudson is one of my favourite people to have been involved in the Victorian railways. I kind of want to write an entire book to tell the story of George Hudson, to show the secrets behind the life of the railway king. (That was his nickname)

You know what? I am going to write a book about George Hudson, if you're reading this in the future it might already be out? Maybe give it a traditional internet search to see.

With that in mind I'll give you the short version of Hudson here as an appetite whetter.

He was the son of a farmer and sadly orphaned by the age of 8. He moved to York at the age of 18 and became an apprentice at Bell and Nicolson which was a draper's shop. I'm going to guess he was pretty good at his job because in 1821 he married his boss's daughter Elizabeth Nicolson. Bell retired and the company became Nicolson and Hudson and by the time 1827 dawned the draper's business was one of the most successful in York.

He became extremely wealthy in 1827 when his great uncle left him £27,000, the Victorian equivalent of winning millions in the lottery. He did receive it in suspicious circumstances as he was thought to have had very little to do with his uncle until he learnt of his illness. We'll probably never know the truth but what is fact is Hudson became one of the richest men in the local area.

He broke into the world of politics in 1832 when he became the treasurer of the York Conservative Party. His political career would see him be an MP for Sunderland between 1845 to 1859 and be elected Lord Mayor of York 3 times in 1837, 38 & 46.

In the early 1830's, a York businessman named James Meek brought together all the important business folk of York and proposed that York needed a railway. Meek owned a glass making company so wanted to take advantage of the cheap coal which could be bought in by the rail. He was basically laughed out the room. Hudson, however, thought it was a good idea. Over the next few years as more successful railways began to spring up the business heads of York were convinced a railway in York was a good idea.

Hudson became treasurer of the York and North Midland Railway company in 1835 and hatched a plan for a railway which could connect York to the Midland railway. He was also instrumental in convincing George Stephenson, who he met in Whitby, to build his new proposed line between London and Newcastle to go through York rather than Leeds.

There was no stopping Hudson and, at the height of his powers in 1844, he was in charge of over 1,000 miles of railway track- which would have been roughly one-fifth in Britain at that time. His wallet was bulging. He was such a heavy weight he apparently told Prince Albert (Queen Victoria's husband) he was a fool.

By 1846 he controlled a quarter of the country's railways and everything he touched seemed to turn to gold. He could do no wrong in the eyes of investors and was known to have saved railway companies which were in financial turmoil. If Hudson, by the now the railway king, bought shares in a company then everyone wanted to buy shares in that company.

In 1848 profits started to drop and questions were starting to be asked about Hudson. He was found to be fiddling finances to suit himself. He'd buy shares from one of his companies for £1 (as an example) then sell them on to another of his companies for £2. People were obviously annoyed, and the country turned on him.

He was forced to repay vast sums of money to the companies he'd swindled but he could never rebuild the trust which had been destroyed. Because he was still an MP, he wasn't thrown into debtors' prison and after he lost the election in 1859, he fled to France to avoid jail.

He returned to Britain in 1865 when it was suggested he could win the election to become MP in Whitby. It was a gamble which didn't pay off and he was thrown in debtors' prison in York and London- not at the same time.

He was freed from jail and was provided for by his remaining friends who managed to pay him £600 of a year to survive on. He and his wife lived in a small house in London.

Hudson died in 1871 with very little money to his name. Hudson had been made by the rails and ultimately, they had destroyed him. Perhaps saddest of all though, his wax model at Madame Tussauds had been melted down. For a man who had had everything, he passed away with less than £200 to his name.

He made a final journey by train to be buried in Scrayingham- which was close to his place of birth.

In York today there's George Hudson Street to remember the man who made York an epicentre of the railway world. After his downfall they had renamed the street Railway Street in order to kick a man whilst he was down, but they changed it back in 1971, on the 100th anniversary of the railway king's death.

Richard Trevithick

I really feel sorry for Richard Trevithick. He's pretty much the guy that everyone always forgets about. He did, however, play an incredibly important role in the birth of the industrial revolution. Have no doubt, Trevithick is the true "father of the railways". He sadly didn't have a lot of business sense which was ultimately his downfall.

Trevithick was born in Cornwall on the 13th of April 1771 and like most genius's seem to, struggled in to stay focused in school. It really says something about the education system that apparently no genius can focus on schoolwork.

He started his professional career in the mining industry like his father before him. He became an engineer at the Ding Dong Mine (yes- that's what it was actually called- it's in Cornwall) in 1797 and became working on high pressure steam engines.

1797 was a good year for Trevithick as it was also the year he married his wife, Jane. The two went on to have six children together. One of his sons, Francis, was amongst the first locomotive engineers on the London and North-western Railway. Engineering seems to run in the family- one of his grandchildren went to Egypt to work on the railways over there.

High pressured steam engines had never been used before. Those who came before were obsessed with the idea of only using low-pressure steam. Their main argument? Low-pressure steam was safer. There is little argument to suggest low-pressure steam engines were safer- but they had next to no power. They wouldn't have been able to hold up the industrial revolution.

He built a full-sized high-pressure steam road vehicle in 1801 and christened it "Puffing Devil" – I'm no marketing expert but I feel like when you're introducing a new technology to the world you should avoid using the word "devil" in it. Perhaps "Puffing Safe and sound" – I told you I was rubbish at marketing.

On Christmas Eve 1801 he pulled six passengers up Camborne Hill. This is what inspired the Cornish folk song "Camborne Hill." I've never personally heard it, but I bet it's a real winner.

As Trevithick continued to test his new steam carriage, he broke it when he crashed into a big hole in the road. He parked it in a shelter with the fire still crackling away. We already know what happens when all the water goes. Puffing Devil exploded.

Again, I'm no expert but if you're trying to convince people high-pressure steam is the future- not calling it anything to do with devil would be the first step- then not having it blow up would be the second step. It was a marketing nightmare.

NOT SO ROMANTIC NEWS

Ride the newly invented steam carriage the "PUFFING DEVIL" – inventor Richard Trevithick says it will get you to 10,000 locations at the same time!"

So, Puffing Devil had an explosive end, but Trevithick stated it was "user error" and not a problem with high pressured steam. People laughed back then- but he wasn't wrong. He did build another steam carriage in 1803 called the "London Steam Carriage" which he used for a round trip in London from Holborn to Paddington and back again.

The reviews for the LSC were bad, the passengers declared it was uncomfortable, and it was really expensive to run compared to horse-drawn carriages, so the steam carriage was left abandoned. It didn't explode though so small steps of improvement.

You'll soon realise that luck wasn't on Trevithick's side. In 1803 one of his high-pressure steam engines exploded in Greenwich and 4 men were killed. Again, Trevithick pleaded operational error, but his rivals (including the pesky James Watt) never stopped jumping up and down about the accident. It seemed everything was going against Trevithick.

In 1805 he travelled up to Newcastle to oversee the building of a locomotive in Tyneside. It was here he almost definitely met

George Stephenson. This particular locomotive ran on wooden rails which kept breaking under the weight of the steam locomotive which led the mine owners to declare that it would be cheaper to keep feeding the horses than to constantly replace the wooden rails every time they snapped.

During this visit to Tyneside, you can bet your shoelaces that George Stephenson will have been watching Trevithick's every move, learning everything he could about the steam locomotive. I think we would have had a very different industrial revolution if Trevithick had never been asked to make a steam locomotive in Newcastle.

Now a resident of London, Trevithick opened his steam circus in 1808. The steam circus was a circular length of track which people could pay to travel around. He ran his brand-new steam locomotive 'Catch Me Who Can'. This is the first recorded instance of passengers paying to travel behind a steam locomotive.

The steam circus wasn't the smash hit Trevithick thought it would be and the revolution of the steam locomotive wasn't gaining any sort of pace so in 1816 Trevithick took a chance and travelled to South America.

His first stop was Peru where he helped build engines to drain water from the silver mines and became a mining advisor for the government. Like seems to be a common occurrence, the money dried up (I'm not sure if that was a pun or not- I'll say pun intended just to be safe).

He did manage to obtain permission to do some mining for himself but because of tensions within Peru with the Spanish he was forced to abandon copper and silver ore on a ship. It is suggested this ore was worth roughly £5500 back in the 1800's.

The Peru plan fell apart for Trevithick, so he travelled to Costa Rica and arrived there in 1822 with a grand plan to revolutionise the mining system. His first plan was to build a railway line to transport mining equipment and resources that came from the mines themselves.

The route he chose quite quickly turned out to the be the wrong one. The first part of the journey would be to use the Juan

River. When the party set out to travel the route it went from bad to worse. One party member drowned and Trevithick himself had to be saved from an alligator attack and drowning.

Trevithick moved onto Columbia where he met Robert Stephenson who was travelling back to Newcastle after his own failed exploits in the mining industry. The two had very little in common, mostly because the last time they'd met Robert had been a little baby, but despite their differences Robert lent Trevithick the £50 it would cost for him to get back home to Britain.

The two parted ways, a sort of metaphorical passing of the torch. Stephenson went to New York (where he nearly drowned) and Trevithick returned home. He may have had a plan to one day return to South America and finish what he started. But he never did.

Once Trevithick returned from South America in 1827, he had lost the race of trying to convince the world about his steam locomotives as the Stephenson's had pulled out into the lead and Geroge Stephenson in particular was claiming a lot of the credit which Trevithick deserved.

His inventing days weren't quite over however as in 1830 he invented a room heater.

In 1833 Trevithick was taken ill with pneumonia and sadly passed away in a Bull hotel in Dartford on the 22nd of April. He died with no money and few friends but, because grave robbing was a popular past time in 1833, his ex-colleagues paid for a night watchman to guard his grave.

Sadly, Trevithick is never remembered in the high regard he should deserve. His adventures alone could make a whole book (nudge nudge, wink wink) and no matter the outcome he played an important part in the creation of the industrial revolution.

I think Trevithick is really interesting and should be talked about a lot but my goodness his surname is hard to type out- I think I spelt it wrong every time I wrote it – and you'll see I wrote it a lot...

George Stephenson

Ah, the "father of the railways". I've got to be honest, I'm not really sure he fully deserved this title. It's obvious that George Stephenson had a brain, but his real superpower was taking everyone else's ideas and combining them to make a finished product. This takes a certain degree of engineering knowhow. I'm definitely not suggesting old George wasn't a good engineer. It's more that he claimed a lot of ideas that weren't his own.

Well actually let's explore that for just a brief paragraph. I've said a lot that George claimed a lot of other people's ideas as his own, but really it wasn't George who claimed the ideas were his- it was everyone else that said he'd come up with all the ideas. George just never denied it. Do you think you'd deny it? He'd been made rich, had great standing in the country- if you were in his shoes would be eager to pass the credit onto everyone else?

An interesting train (pun intended) of thought to maybe think about when you're settling down surfing the internet to see which ideas you can combine to make your millions.

George Stephenson was born on the 9th of June 1781 in a place called Wylan which is just 10 miles west of Newcastle.

He had two children- Robert Stephenson who went onto be just almost as famous as his father and a daughter (born 1805) who sadly died a few weeks after being born.

Stephenson's first claim to fame was at the end of 1815 when he created a new miner's lamp which is called the Geordie Lamp. In the mines explosions caused by flames and gas were common so the Geordie Lamp was built with glass around the flame. If the flame went out, then it meant there was harmful gasses close by and the miners themselves had more time to get out of danger.

A really good invention which most likely saved plenty of lives. But even this caused some controversy as the Geordie Lamp had a lot of similarities to the Davy Lamp which had been invented by Humphry Davy in the same year. Do you think Stephenson had already started borrowing other people's ideas? I'll leave you to make up your own mind.

He may have been good at gaining credit by combining lots of different ideas, but Stephenson was amongst the first to realise that a connected railway network was the best way forward so started to build all his tracks the same width apart (gauge). So he became champion of the "standard gauge" which was 4ft 8 inches across. This had been the same width as the old trackways the horses had used.

It is no secret that George struggled when Robert decided to try his luck in America. The fact he couldn't read or write suddenly became more of an issue and between the two of them it was Robert who was the true businessman. George had little knowledge of how to sell ideas, which almost certainly caused him to make a pig's ear of his meeting in parliament when presenting the original proposal for the Liverpool to Manchester Railway route.

He passed away on the 12th of August 1848 of something called pleurisy. I've tried to understand what this disease is for about six months- I'm still none the wiser so I'll leave it to you to find out for yourselves.

Magnus Volk

I'm not a betting sorta person but I'd bet good money you've never heard of Magnus Volk before. He was born on the 19th of October 1851 in Brighton, on the English south coast. He was a keen inventor from a young age and was fascinated with electricity.

He bought the first telephone system to Brighton in 1879. He installed it in his house and also installed one for his friend. He loved being first and he was the first person on the south coast to fit electric lights in his house in 1880.

His fame came from his railways. He built a small narrow-gauge line along the Brighton seafront and blew everyone's mind when he powered it with electricity. The first electric railway in the country. This line is still in operation today and is, unsurprisingly, the oldest electric railway in the world.

This railway wasn't the first electric railway in the world it was more likely the fourth behind Miller's line which opened in 1875 in Russia, Werner Von Siemen's 1879 build Berlin line and a second line which opened in Berlin in 1881- Berlin is a well-known city- but I bet none of you knew it was a leader in the electric railways. - I didn't either so don't worry, but at this point you'll have realised that knowing more than me isn't that difficult.

His main claim to fame was creating the Pioneer, nicknamed Daddy-Long-Legs, which ran in the sea off the coast of Brighton. It ran in shallow waters at very slow speeds but was a popular spectacular when it first ran in 1896. Sadly, it closed in 1901.

He built a three-wheeled electric carriage in 1887 before deciding three wheels weren't enough and building a four-wheeled electric carriage the year after in 1888. The four-wheeled electric carriage was actually ordered by the sultan of the Ottoman Empire.

Magnus passed away on the 20th of May 1937 in Brighton. Once a Brighton lad- always a Brighton lad.

Teachers are wrong

I have a mind-blowing truth to tell you. Teachers don't know everything. Some of them might act like that do. Here are some things that even teachers get wrong about the railways. Use them to help correct them but remember- don't make them cry, everyone makes mistakes at the end of the day.

#1-Rocket was the first ever steam locomotive

A lot of teachers will tell you that Stephenson's Rocket was the first steam locomotive ever built. This is wrong! Zero points rewarded. The first steam locomotive was actually built by Richard Trevithick in 1804.

#2- Steam locomotives have steering wheels

I wish I could say this next one was a joke, but I once heard a teacher tell his students that trains had steering wheels. I know the teacher wasn't joking because when I explained trains didn't have steering wheels, he was the most shocked of them all. Let's put this to bed once and for all. Steam locomotives do not have steering wheels.

#3- Steam locomotives have a diesel engine in case they break down.

No word of a lie I have heard a teacher say this. These are the people responsible for teaching the next generation and they're telling their students that steam locomotives had a diesel engine in case they broke down. This of course, is complete nonsense. Steam locomotives did not have diesel engines in case they broke down.

#4- James Watt invented the steam engine.

This one is an easy thing to get wrong as there are still textbooks in schools that say the Scottish inventor did invent the steam engine. It is wrong to say Watt invented the steam engine but right to say he improved the steam engine. He made them more efficient, amongst other things- oh and by steam engine I mean a stationary engine powered by steam.

#5- George Stephenson invented the steam locomotive

Ha-ha-ha-ha-ha-ha-ha. I think I've knocked Stephenson down enough pegs in this book. You know by now that Richard Trevithick invented the steam locomotive. I make it everyone's mission to help spread the word about Trevithick.

#6- The Rainhill trails took place over one day

In fairness this should also be labelled Andy is wrong. Most other books neglect to mention that the Rainhill Trials took place over 9 days of competition. It ran from the 6th-14th October 1829.

#7- The railways were romantic

Sigh! If you hear your teacher say this please buy them this book- and ask them to leave a review. There's a law that says teachers always have to leave a 5-star review... I promise.

#8 Steam locomotives had an electric motor in case they broke down.

Please refer to #3 – the answer is the same, but you have to switch the word diesel with electric.

The locomotives in this book (and some that aren't)

Rocket
Designed by Robert and George Stephenson and winner of the Rainhill trials in 1829. It reached a dazzling speed of 30 mph. You can see it today in the National Railway Museum.

Locomotion No 1
Built to run on the Stockton and Darlington railway. It hauled the first train on the new railway in September 1825 and exploded in 1828. It was rebuilt and ran until 1850 before being converted into a stationary engine. It was preserved in 1857.

Catch Me Who Can
The final steam locomotive that came from the brain of Richard Trevithick. Catch Me Who Can was the first locomotive to pull paying passengers at Trevithick's steam circus in the early 1800's. It reached speeds of a dizzying 12 mph and helped prove that iron rails were the future for the railways.

Cyloped
Not a steam locomotive but this horse powered competitor in the Rainhill trials would have been a sight to see. It was designed by Thomas Shaw Brandreth.

Novelty
The world's first tank engine and another competitor of the Rainhill trials. It was the crowd's favourite as it looked most like a steam carriage but a burst water pipe aw the end of its race. It was designed by John Ericsson and John Braithwaite.

Perseverance
The Scottish locomotive that was built by John Reed Hill and Timothy Burstall to compete in the Rainhill trials. Sadly, the lack of rails between Scotland and Liverpool put an end to its race before

it really started as it kept falling off the transport on route to Liverpool.

Sans Pareil
The Rainhill trails competitor built by Timothy Hackworth. During the trails it was going well until there was an issue with its cylinders. There was uproar as the Robert Stephenson & Co factory had manufactured some cylinders for Sans Pareil. Foul play couldn't be proved, however, as lots of cylinders from lots of places were made, so we'll never know which ones were used.

Pioneer
All right not technically a steam locomotive but worth a spot in this section. The electric carriage on wheels which ran through the shallow waters in Brighton.

Pen-y-Darren
A Trevithick built locomotive built in 1804. It was a locomotive that made the first ever steam powered railway journey when it travelled 9 miles – Do you really need any more evidence that Richard Trevithick was the true father of the railway?

Puffing Devil
Another not a steam locomotive entry but an important part of the history of the industrial revolution and the steam locomotives. Puffing Devil was a high-pressured steam carriage built by Richard Trevithick. It pulled passengers up Cambourne Hill in 1801 before blowing up after further testing.

Fairy Queen
The Fairy Queen was built in Leeds in 1855. It was swiftly shipped to India to haul mail trains. During the Indian Rebellion, 1857, it would also pull troop trains. Once it stopped running in 1909 it spent the next 30 years outside Howrah Station on a pedestal and was moved to the Railway training school in 1943.
The Fairy Queen was given heritage status in 1972 and given pride and place at the National Rail Museum in New Delhi., It was then returned to full working order in 1997.

Big fancy words and what they mean

Most authors would call this a glossary. I am not like most authors. So here are the big fancy words in this book and what they mean.

Steam Locomotive parts

Regulator

The regulator is just like the accelerator in a car. To speed up the driver would lift up the regulator. To slow down the driver would lower the regulator.

Reverser

This is basically the steam locomotives gear stick. Depending which way it is turned before you set off decides if you're going to go forward or backwards.

Brakes

No explanation needed. They help the locomotives stop- eventually.

Tender

The trailer on the back of the larger locomotives. It's where the coal and water needed for the journey were stored.

Firebox

Speaks for itself. The firebox is where the fireman shovels the coal and makes a fire. The heat of the fire travels through the locomotive and boils the water. (Along with cooking breakfast and burning poo.)

Boiler

This is where the water is. It comes from the Tender and is heated up by the hot air which travels through long tubes from the firebox.

Wheels

Big round things.

Pistons

These connect from the cylinders to the wheels. As the steam pushes them backward and forwards, they turn the wheels around.

Chimney

Where the used steam and the hot air comes out of.

Smokebox

The bit of the locomotive that's behind the front (bit that looks like a clock face). The crew use this to cook food in, but it also gathers ash and has to be cleaned out by the cleaners.

Cab

The place where the driver and fireman worked. In the early days they wouldn't have any seats, walls, or roofs.

Ashpan

The ashpan sits underneath the firebox. As the fires got bigger and hotter the smaller flakes of ash started to set fire to any plants or grass at the side of the tracks.

Railway terminology

Gauge

The width of the track. Standard Gauge or Stephenson's Gauge as it was sometimes known was 4ft 8 ½ inches wide. Many railways around the world use this Gauge today.

Rolling stock

The locomotives, carriages and all other vehicles that are used on the railways.

Points
Pretty much the junctions on the railways. They decide if you're travelling left, right, or just going straight on.

Signals
The traffic lights of the railway world.

Shunting
Shunting is organising carriages and other rolling stock.

Express train
The fast trains on the tracks. Express trains are normally the ones travelling longer distances- like the modern Edinburgh to London.

Freight train
A train pulling no passengers and carrying things like coal or other materials.

Local trains
Slower moving trains going shorter distances.

Parts of the railway track

Rail
The iron or steel rail sits on top of the track, it is what the wheels of the trains sit on.

Fish plates
Annoying they don't look like fish. They are used to bolt two bits of rail together.

Sleepers
The mostly wooden planks which the rail rests upon. They are used to support the rail. They are used to stop the rail moving away from each other.

Chair

Even the railway gets tried. The chairs are often called lots of different things, but I've always called them chairs. They are on the sleepers and the rail sits in them.

Ballast

The stones you see at the bottom of the whole track. It was put down to ensure the track was level.

Thankyou

You did it! You got to the end of the book! High- fives all around!

Thank you so much for reading my first venture into the world of non-fiction, I hope you enjoyed reading it as much as I've enjoyed writing it and I do like to think you may have learned a thing or two reading this book.

I have a lot more not-so-romantic railway books planned so make sure you keep your ears to the ground for release dates. I'm aiming to have at least one new edition out every year so fingers crossed I can manage it.

I'd like to place on record my thanks to the poor souls who had to read this book to help me find all the spelling and grammar errors in the book. You really paid the price for me not listening in English lessons at school. My heartfelt thanks go out to James and Emma.

Thanks for going through the book with a fine toothpick and making sure I said trail instead of trial. Thank you! (I also might have written this wrong to annoy you or just fluked going it right).

There are too many people to name but just to say a quick thank you to everyone who has taught me anything about the railways over the years- I'm now pulling a George Stephenson and combining everyone else's ideas to make this book.

A big thanks to those who have provided artwork for the book. The drawings are incredible and add so much to this unromantic journey. Modelsta, Mwkhoirul and Ayasuarjaya are all available on Fiverr and I can't recommend them enough.

I designed the cover myself- so go me!

If you've enjoyed this book, please consider checking out my other book- "The Vampire Fairy" which follows the adventures of Phoenix as he's transported to a forest where the sun never rises and a vampire stalks the land. The Vampire Fairy is very different to the not so romantic railways, in fact it has no railways in it. But if you fancy some fiction with your cake then please consider checking it out.

Whilst I'm self-advertising, I have my own YouTube channel called "Andy's Kitchen Show" where I explore lots of different subjects in a fun manner to make educational videos that are

hopefully more entertaining than the stuff you endure at school. If you fancy some cool videos, then please head across to YouTube, and check out my channel.

Once again, a big thank you to everyone who has read the book and supported me in anyway. I truly appreciate it. Don't forget to leave a review on Amazon and I'll hopefully see you in another one really soon.

At the end of our journey together I hope you've learnt at least something but most importantly I hope you remember the most important lesson of this book.

The railways were not so romantic after all.

F.S: (Funny story).

The picture of the elephant running on a treadmill in the first chapter is only there because I wrote "Elephant" instead of "horse" when I ordered the drawing. I was too embarrassed to change it.

Printed in Great Britain
by Amazon